Vedanta

in Light of

Christian Wisdom

Vedanta

in Light of

Christian Wisdom

Wolfgang Smith

Philos-Sophia Initiative Foundation

Copyright © 2022 Wolfgang Smith

All rights reserved. No part of this book may be reproduced or used in any manner without the prior written permission of the copyright owner, except for the use of brief quotations in a book review.

To request permission, contact the publisher at
info@philossophiainitiative.com

ISBN: 979-8-9851470-1-8

Library of Congress Control Number: 2022902752

Philos-Sophia Initiative Foundation
www.philos-sophia.org

*An die Seligste Jungfrau Maria,
Mutter vom grossem Sieg*

TABLE OF CONTENTS

	Introduction	1
1.	Christianity and the Vedic Tradition	7
2.	From Benedictine to *Sādhu*: The Case of Henri Le Saux	41
3.	*Extra Ecclesiam Nulla Salus*	61
4.	Breaking the *Ātma-Māyā* Dichotomy	73
5.	Logocentric Metaphysics	89
	Postscript	101
	Glossary	105
	Index	109

INTRODUCTION

This book has evolved out of an article on "Christianity and the Vedic Tradition," which became the first chapter. But let me start at the beginning, which goes back about three-quarters of a century.

I was a student at Cornell—majoring in physics, mathematics, and philosophy—when I came across Rabindranath Tagore's *Gitanjali*, his "Little Song" for which he received a Nobel Prize. And the very first stanza swept me off my feet:

> *Thou hast made me endless, such is thy pleasure...*
> *At the immortal touch of thy hands my little heart loses its*
>   *limits in joy*
> *and gives birth to utterance ineffable.*

Most certainly I had not heard anything like that from my mentors at Cornell. It touched me deeply, and aroused in my soul what the poet terms "intimations of immortality." And although I continued with my physics, mathematics, and even the so-called philosophy, it would never again be the same. In the wake of that first "*Thou has made me endless,*" I knew something was missing in my life, and sensed that it was indeed "*the one thing needful.*"

I did not of course stop with Rabindranath Tagore. Soon thereafter I came upon Sri Ramakrishna, the great nineteenth-century Bengali master. And when he declared that the purpose of human life was what the translator termed "the realization of God"—I was convinced. Before long I made contact with a Hindu monastic order founded by Swami Vivekananda, a disciple of Sri Ramakrishna, and began henceforth to see the world through Vedic eyes.

On a few occasions I did bring up what I deemed to be pearls of Vedic wisdom in conversation with my professors. I recall one exchange in particular, in which I tried to explain to Prof. Max Black—a leading light in the field of "analytic philosophy"—that there is a state, accessible through yogic means, in which the separation between man and God appears to be transcended. And to this day I remember his response: "I do not deny that this may be the greatest experience—but it can have nothing to do with truth." In an instant my interest in "analytic philosophy" plunged to zero.

I managed in due time to find my bearings in keeping with my new orientation. Physics and mathematics would do fine as an occupation, I concluded: there are fascinating questions here, and the beauty is that, notwithstanding our metaphysical ignorance, they can apparently be answered by intellectual means at our disposal. And when I began to sense that this may not actually hold true in the case of physics—that here too philosophy of a more than "analytic" kind may be called for—the die was cast: I would take my doctorate in "pure" mathematics. It proved to be one of the best decisions I ever made: I can see in retrospect that it was for me the only way to survive an academic career.

Getting back to my early days: the longer I pursued my Vedic aspirations, the more deeply persuaded I became that there are men in India—and for that matter, women too[1]—who actually had attained knowledge of an ultimate kind: a knowledge not of "the ten thousand things," but of *"the one thing,"* rather, *"by the knowing of which all things are known"* as a Vedic passage has it. And this surmise came to be decisively confirmed in 1960, after I had obtained my doctorate, when I left MIT to sojourn seven months in India, living as best I could amidst *sādhus*: Hindu monks accustomed to spend most of their days and nights in spheres, the very existence of which is unknown in the West.

∽

The story does not however end with this recognition. Years later, after I had settled into a rather comfortable existence as a professor of mathematics, a young woman came to our Department to earn a Ph.D. She was beautiful, cultured, and Christian to the core; and after her graduation we were married. I relate this because it is crucial to the story: it was namely through the silent and spiritually uplifting influence of Thea that I returned at last to my Christian roots.

Two books helped to tip the scale: a biography of St. Catherine of Siena—which enabled me to glimpse the unearthly beauty of this magnificent saint—and St. Augustine's commentary on the Gospel of St. John, which shed light upon the Christian Eschaton. The instant I sensed the categorical difference between the Vedantic "merging in *brahman*" and the Christian union

---

1. One of the most highly enlightened personages in India at the time was a woman named Anandamayi Ma: mighty *sādhus* bowed low at her feet.

with *God the Father mediated by Jesus Christ*, I realized that I am "incurably" Christian after all. Whether it be the Catholic baptism I received as a child or my spiritual DNA, the issue was henceforth closed.

What did not however end is my profound respect for the Vedic religion. I can never forget the great *sādhus* I have been privileged to meet, and the spiritual gifts they occasionally bestowed upon me, somewhat as if tossing sweets to a child. The one thing in my favor was that I approached these sages with deep reverence: with "folded hands" as it were—and it appears they responded in kind.

∽

Getting back to my article on "Christianity and the Vedic Tradition": the wonder is that I waited all these years to write it! There are key questions, namely, that present themselves as soon as one reflects upon the relation between the two traditions. Leaving out of consideration uninformed or narrowly sectarian opinions, it appears that the current trend among knowledgeable authorities is in effect to view Christianity through Vedantic eyes. By the time however I had half completed my reflections, I came to recognize that *the truth of Christianity cannot* in fact *be comprehended in Vedantic terms*. At the same time it dawned on me that the reductionists based their conclusion upon the contrast between Vedanta—the *non plus ultra* of the Vedic tradition—and Christianity *as conceived on a more or less "exoteric" plane*. In terms of the Pauline metaphor, the doctrine of "Vedantic primacy" rests thus upon a comparison between "*milk*" on the Christian side, and "*red meat*" on the other, the outcome of which was never in doubt.

To make abundantly clear that the issue is more than "academic," I added what is now chapter 2, which tells the story of a French Benedictine monk, named Henri Le Saux, who came to India in 1948, had a brief encounter with a Hindu master, and taking the name of Swami Abhishiktananda, began himself to practice *yoga* in barren caves. And whereas I am filled with admiration at his capacity to scale the sheer "rock-face of Mt. Everest," I have reservations regarding the perception of Christianity at which he arrived. Abhishiktananda presupposes two tenets, which in my opinion invalidate what he has to say: first, that the Christian Eschaton—known as *Salvation*—coincides with the Vedantic, a terminus I refer as the *nirvānic* option; and secondly, that one can grasp the nature of Christianity "from the outside," and in particular, from a Vedantic point of vantage. My outlook differs thus from that of Swami Abhishiktananda in that I categorically deny both of these assumptions.

Following this encounter with the French Benedictine-turned-*sādhu*, I made it my aim to compare the two religions objectively, without looking at either through the lenses of the other. What ultimately permits us to do so is a stunning metaphysical exegesis, discovered by Meister Eckhart, that enables one to comprehend the Vedantic "*māyā*" in terms indigenous to Christianity. By means of this Eckhartian masterstroke—tantamount to the discovery of a "Christian yoga"—it becomes possible, for the first time, to compare the ultimate "trans-*māyā*" metaphysics of Vedanta with that of Christianity objectively; and the result proves to be enlightening in the extreme. What reduces namely to *ātma* on the side of Vedanta corresponds precisely to what Christianity knows as the Trinity.

Here then is the key that enables us to comprehend the difference between the two religions: it is the *Logos*—the Second Person of the Trinity—that ultimately breaks the *ātma-māyā* dichotomy, and in so doing gives rise to an Eschaton inconceivable in Vedic terms. What enables man "*to see God and live*" is the mediation of Christ: "*the Word*" that "*was made flesh and dwelt among us.*"

At the end of this inquiry one finds not only that the relation between Christianity and the Vedic tradition has been radically clarified, but that by way of the Eckhartian exegesis an ultimate engagement with Christian metaphysics has been initiated.

Wolfgang Smith
February 9, 2022

1

CHRISTIANITY AND THE VEDIC TRADITION

An assertion made reputedly by Hans Urs von Balthasar has intrigued me for a long time. As Scott Randall Paine states by way of summary, "the Christian West's engagement with India would rival its ancient engagement with Greece":[1] what are we to make of this? For a Christian there is of course no question what it might be that "India" has to gain from such an encounter; what may come as a surprise, on the other hand, is that the "Christian West" too may have something to receive. The Vedic heritage appears to be the oldest spiritual tradition in the world, antedating the Judeo-Christian; and as I recall from multiple sojourns in India—which by now, howbeit, go back more than half a century—that tradition was yet very much alive. You needed but to make your way to Hardwar on the upper Ganges, an ancient site flanked by the foothills of the Himalayas, to encounter Vedic[2] monks: one can recognize them at a glance by the *gerua* color of their robe.

---

1. From his preface to *A Catholic Mind Awake: The Writings of Bernard Kelly* (Angelico Press, 2017), p. ii.
2. I find the adjective "Vedic" preferable to the word "Hindu," which derives simply from the name of the Indus river.

What, then, might it be these *sādhus* seek? As it happens, the *gerua* itself gives us a clue: it is the color of fire, after all. And in a land which burns the bodies of its dead, the symbolism is unmistakable: the *gerua* color of the *sādhu*'s robe proclaims that his body—his worldly being—has already been consigned to the flames. What is it, then, for the sake of which that ultimate sacrifice is offered? And how, above all, does that Vedic Eschaton relate to the Christian: that is the central question we propose to ponder.

What we have to say in this chapter breaks into four parts. In the first, we shall contrast the two religions—the Vedic and the Christian—to reveal the profundity of their difference. In the second, we propose to exhibit their common elements to reveal a deep kinship. In the third, we shall ponder Meister Eckhart's conception of what may quite rigorously be termed a "Christian yoga." And in the fourth part we shall explain why it is by no means needful to understand a word of what we said in the previous three.

I

To obviate from the start a not altogether unlikely misconception, let me touch briefly upon the subject of "paganism." The word itself appears to have been coined in reference to "pagan" cults such as those extant in the Mediterranean regions in early Christian times. Now these were, properly speaking, degenerate vestiges of inherently polytheistic religions which had flourished in these lands in a bygone age; and whatever may be said of these erstwhile beliefs and practices, the fact is that such religions do have a tendency to decay and become eventually "demonized."³ In my edition of the *Stromata* by Clement of Alexandria,⁴ the chapter descriptive of pagan rituals is left untranslated, presumably because it might prove nauseous to the contemporary reader. To put this subject to rest, suffice it to say emphatically that one thing, at least, the Vedic religion is not: it is, most certainly, *not* a paganism.

Getting back to the *sādhu*'s quest, one might say that he is striving to purify his body and mind, seeking to still the ceaseless welling of thoughts and emotions. More precisely: what authentic *sādhus* "do" is practice *yoga*, based upon teachings passed down through the ages, from master to disciple. The Sanskrit term itself is cognate to our word *yoke*, and signifies a union of some kind: in this instance, presumably, between man and God—reminiscent of our word "religion," given that it stems from *re-ligare*, "binding back." And whereas that yogic union itself cannot be described, the methodology of *yoga* can, and has in fact been set forth in its essence in the opening sentence of the definitive text.⁵ *Yoga*, declares Patanjali, is "*chittavrittinirodha*": the "uprooting" (*nirodha*) of mental (*chitta*) modifications (*vritti*). Think of the mind as an ocean: *yoga* is then the stilling of its waves.

---

3. St. Paul informs us of this repeatedly, for instance in 1 Cor. 10:20.

4. It may be worthy of note that when Pantaenus gave up his position as head of the Alexandrian Academy (which he passed on to his disciple Clement around the year 200), he was said to be on his way—yes: to India.

5. Traditionally taken to be the *Yoga Sutras* of Patanjali.

As to the prophesied encounter between the Christian West and India: it may be time for each side—the Christian and the Vedic—to understand the other to the extent, at least, that a religion *can* be understood "from the outside." For the Christian this means to catch a first glimpse, presumably, of what inspires the Vedic *sādhu* to live a life of poverty and chastity, practicing austerities undreamed of even in our most ascetic monasticism. And let me add—for those who might shrug this off as "pious exaggeration"—that I myself have witnessed *sādhus* spending their days and nights in deep meditation, and have caught a glimpse of the ensuing "serenity"—for lack of a better term—which struck me as patently *supernatural*.

I recall a comment made, quite casually, by one of these adepts, which I seem to grasp better today than I did at the time. "*We are striving to enter the abode of death*" he said, "*and they ask us to write books!*" The "they," to be sure, refers to "westernized" individuals who seek their wisdom in the printed word; but what exactly does it mean "*to enter the abode of death*"? Years later I learned that the teachings of Parmenides derive likewise, according to tradition, from that "abode of death." It appears that the illustrious pre-Socratic was not in truth a "philosopher" in the now customary sense: not a person who *thinks*, but someone, rather, who has actually "stopped thinking," someone in fact who has consummated the yogic *nirodha* and entered that "*abode*" where "thinking" comes ultimately to an end.[6] And I would add that, strange as this may seem to the "westernized" observer, it is *de jure* not surprising in the least: one needs but to recall that Socrates himself—the father, if you will, of Occidental philosophy—characterized that discipline as *"the practice of death."*[7]

~

A religion is in a way defined by its Eschaton: the supreme End it sets before its votaries; and when it comes to the Vedic, we shall refer to that Eschaton as the *"nirvānic"* option. Though of Buddhist origin, the term—which literally signifies a "blowing out," as of a candle flame—strikes me as optimal in that it vividly conveys what appears to be the graspable idea: a veritable "extinction" of the "human" as such, to the point where there *is* no more human "I." That Eschaton proves thus to be conceivable only in terms of what it is not, in keeping with the traditional *"neti, neti"*—"not so, not so"—of the Vedic texts. Let us remember: *yoga* is, after all, *chittavrittinirodha*.

---

6. It appears that Parmenides was the recipient of a yogic tradition associated with the Phoenicians, which they disseminated throughout the Mediterranean regions. It is conceivable that the so-called *hesychast* tradition—which is indeed inherently yogic, and is extant to this day among the monastic communities of Mount Athos—stems from that source. For more on Parmenides and his connection with India, see my chapter *"Cakra* and Planet: O. M. Hinze's Discovery" in *Science & Myth* (Angelico Press, 2010). See also Peter Kingsley's masterful treatise entitled *Reality* (Golden Sufi Center Publishing, 2003).

7. *Phaedo* 64a

That ultimate state—which can be known only by way of its attainment—is traditionally designated in the Vedic literature by various names: *moksha*, for instance, meaning "liberation," a setting free. This is however to be understood—not as a liberation *of* the human being—but *from the condition*, rather, *of being human*, which is in a way the very opposite: something, thus, which *ipso facto* eludes our intellectual grasp. Try as we may, there is no way of circumventing the necessity of *yoga*: in the Vedic religion, at least, the "*neti, neti*" always has the last word.

How, then, can we mortals know of that state, that Vedic Eschaton, if its attainment entails a termination of the human messenger? Suffice it to say that it happens, every now and then, that the physical body of a *sādhu* practicing *yoga* survives the attainment of that ultimate realization, in which case we are confronted by what Vedic tradition recognizes as a supreme master or enlightened sage. The historical sage known to the world as Gautama Buddha may doubtless be cited as such a personification of Enlightenment, even though he appears to stand historically outside the Vedic tradition. What confronts us here, however, is not actually a human being, but in a way the very opposite: a *nirvāna* or extinction of one, you might say.

Yet hardly a century passes without the appearance, somewhere upon Indian soil, of such a Master, endowed with the marks of a so-called *jivanmukta* or fully "liberated" sage. By way of example one may cite Sri Ramana Maharshi, the renowned sage of Tiruvannamalai who, in the first half of the twentieth century, became rather well known even in the West. There are books recording his conversations with visitors, illustrated with photographs of the master; yet it is *we* who make these identifications, the point being that an authentic *jivanmukta* does not. In fact, he silently proclaims the very opposite.

Let this much suffice, then, as a first glimpse of the Vedic religion in its supreme manifestation. We have attempted to convey a certain apprehension of its Eschaton the only way it *can be* conveyed: i.e., by affirming in effect what it *is not*. And I surmise that this might indeed prove to be the opening recognition to emerge at that prophesied "engagement with India."

To arrive at an "orthodox" comprehension of the Vedic Eschaton, one needs evidently to consult the primary sources of the Vedic tradition. I have chosen a verse—not from the oldest strata, known as the Upanishads—but from a later work, regarded with almost equal reverence: the Bhagavad Gita namely, which literally means "the Lord's Song." It takes the form of a dialogue between *Arjuna*, a warrior on the eve of battle, and *Krishna* his charioteer, personifying God himself. Here then are the words of Sri Krishna which strike me as, in a way, definitive of the Vedic realization:

> *The unreal never is. The Real never ceases to be. This fact is truly perceived by the seers of Truth.*[8]

"*The unreal never is*": that undoubtedly is key. How, then, are we to understand that "*never is*"? Apparently that so-called "*unreal*"—like the proverbial "*snake in the rope*"[9]—*is* ultimately nothing at all. The crucial point, however, is that this is not a matter of philosophical opinion or mere speculation, but "*is truly perceived by the seers of Truth*": everything hinges upon that! And it is here, precisely, that the *chittavrittinirodha* comes into play, as indeed it must.

From our human point of vantage, of course, that Vedic "*never is*" appears to be counterfactual; yet, for "*the seers of Truth*" the matter stands just the other way round: it is *we* who are deluded, it is we who mistake "*the rope for the snake.*" It is to be noted, moreover, that this Vedic claim can in fact be supported on Judeo-Christian grounds as well: the "*ego sum qui sum*" of Exodus 3:14, for example, which likewise, in a way, reduces our "empirical world" to the category of the "*never is.*"

Our Vedic text distinguishes categorically between the world as normally conceived, and what it terms "*the Real,*" which answers broadly to the conception of God. And it confronts us with a stupendous claim: "*The unreal never is. The Real never ceases to be.*" But whereas this is apt to strike us as a philosophical speculation—and presumably a rather "far out" one at that—the fact is that that the Vedic claim is based, not on human speculation, but upon the *chittavrittinirodha*, precisely. To grasp what the *Gītā* proclaims regarding the *Real* and the *unreal*, one therefore needs at last to accomplish that "rooting out"—that consummate *nirodha*—oneself.

---

9. An Indian expression, based upon the fact that, in semi-darkness, a rope is easily mistaken for a serpent.

∼

Not only, however, is this authentic *yoga* something contemporary man knows nothing about, but it is in fact diametrically opposed to the core tendencies with which he is typically imbued. The very culture and *modus vivendi* of present-day civilization point us in exactly the opposite direction: instead of abating the "mental modifications," we tend to stir them up and keep them running by all possible means. From a yogic perspective, we are heading precisely in the wrong direction: if there be such a thing as an "anti-*yoga*," we surely have mastered it.

What needs moreover to be grasped is the absolute necessity of *discipleship* in the full untruncated sense of that term: there is absolutely no such thing as a "do it yourself" *yoga*. And to comprehend fully what in truth this entails, one is ultimately obliged to assimilate an entire culture. Strictly speaking, of course, discipleship refers to a qualified master or *guru*;[10] yet in premodern India it was, in a way, the entire culture that contributed to the formation of a spiritual aspirant. Here was a civilization molded by the spiritual vision embodied in the oldest scriptures of the world. Every essential of Hindu culture was thus, in some way, expressive of the Vedic ideal as embodied, one might say, in the iconic image of the enlightened Master. He was to be seen throughout premodern India, seated in the lotus posture, with perhaps a faint smile upon his lips: the perfected Sage, who by dint of *yoga* has broken the spell of

---

10. But not, of course, a perfected master or *jivanmukta*, needless to say.

māyā—the deceptions of a half-knowing—to attain an unmediated vision of the ultimate Truth. Such, then, are the contours of the supreme Eschaton, or better said, of the Way to its attainment, set before mankind by the first major religion.

Let us now turn to Christianity, the religion founded, long after the Vedic era, by Jesus Christ. In seemingly diametric opposition to the Vedic, Christ has set before mankind a hitherto unrecognized Eschaton henceforth know as *Salvation*. In place of a *nirvānic* extinction, Christianity offers an immortality in which the "human"—so far from being "blown out" like a candle flame—is actually perfected and "*saved*."

From a Vedic point of vantage it doubtless appears that the Christian Eschaton constitutes something "non-ultimate," as can in fact be said in regard to its own devotional or "*bhaktic*" cults, centered upon what is termed an *ishta devāta*: a "humanized" conception—or manifestation, if you will—of God. The decisive point is that with *the birth of Christ*—the advent of the *Incarnation*—a hitherto nonexistent option has been bestowed upon mankind: *the immortalization*, namely, *of the human person as such*. What was not only impossible but indeed *unthinkable* before the Birth of Christ has become a reality upon His Death. That Christ-given Eschaton—what Christianity denominates *Salvation*—is however achievable only *within the Mystical Body of Christ*, which is in a sense the Church. But it is essential to understand from the outset that *this fact does not in any way "invalidate" the truth of the Vedic religion*, which neither affirms nor denies that Christian Eschaton.

This categorical lack of "conflict," I surmise, may well prove to be one of the prime recognitions to emerge from that encounter prophesied by von Balthasar; and most assuredly, this realization itself would forever change the theological landscape: *rectify it*, I believe. On the one hand, namely, it confirms the ancient dictum *extra ecclesiam nulla salus*[11]—*but without denying the truth of the Vedic religion*! And if I may express an opinion of my own: on that basis Christian missionaries may indeed, in times to come, convert a significant segment of the Vedic faithful: *at long last the message of Christianity can make sense to a believing Hindu*!

We have moved rather quickly to make a central point; it is however to be noted that the categorical discrepancy between the two doctrines—the Vedic and the Christian—calls for reflection of the deepest kind. It is first of all to be noted that the respective scriptures—so far from being contradictory—actually complement and in a way illuminate each other. Let one example suffice: we have indicated that the supreme Enlightenment, as conceived in the Vedic tradition, cannot be attained in the human state, but demands what we have termed the *nirvānic* extinction. I find it profoundly significant that Christianity confirms this fact: as we read in John 1:18: "*No man has seen God at any time.*" The point is that such "*seeing of God*" as is accessible to the

---

11. "Outside the Church there is no salvation."

Christian—be it here or hereafter—proceeds *through Christ*, the Incarnate Logos. One might say that the Blessed "*see God the Father in Jesus Christ the Son*," and that *only thus* can "*man see God.*"

What distinguishes Christianity theologically is, first of all, the root conception of the Trinity, followed by that of the Incarnation. And let us note emphatically that, in all the Vedic scriptures, not a trace of either conception is to be found: both of these quintessentially Christian teachings were revealed to mankind by Jesus Christ. To those, moreover, who might bring up the Hindu notion of "*avatāra*"—often translated as "incarnation"[12]—suffice it to say that there are no words, even, in the Sanskrit language expressive of the Christian sense of that term. Not only are the conceptions of Trinity and Incarnation nowhere to be found in the Vedic scriptures, but it appears, as we have said, that *ante Christum* the *nirvānic* option stood in fact alone as the ultimate Eschaton open in principle to mankind.[13]

What empowers the Christian to attain immortality—*which cannot but consist in an eternal union with God*—without forfeiting human nature derives from the fact that *God himself has assumed that nature in Christ*. It is thus by way of the Incarnate Logos—acting, so to speak, as intermediary—that a "non-*nirvānic*" immortality has been offered to mankind. And let it be noted that Christ Himself confirms this unequivocally,

---

12. Literally, the term "*avatāra*" means "one who has descended," which is not the same as becoming incarnate.

13. Orthodox Hindus might argue that the Vedic religion is open only to Hindus by birth, a point we do not wish to dispute.

in what is known as *"the high priestly prayer,"* by the words:

> *And this is life eternal, that they might know thee the only true God, and Jesus Christ whom thou hast sent.*[14]

It is vital to recognize, however, that this proffered immortality hinges upon what Christianity terms *baptism*: for *it is by way of baptism that we are*—normally at least—*incorporated into the Mystical Body of Christ.*

∼

Contrasting the Christian and the Vedic Eschaton, it is apparent that the two present themselves as in a sense antipodal—somewhat as "a dewdrop slipping into the shining sea" is to a "wedding feast."[15] Whether or not, moreover, the former can in truth be conceived as an "immortality"—other, of course, than that of God himself—strikes me as a question which may admit of no humanly comprehensible answer.[16]

A few words, at least, on the subject of so-called "reincarnation" may be in order to dispel a widespread confusion associated with that notion. The idea, first of all, that the individual soul—the so-called *jiva*—transmigrates after death into another body is not an authentically Vedic tenet. Admittedly there are

---

14. John 17:3
15. The dewdrop metaphor is taken from Edwin Arnold's *The Light of Asia*, his stupendous poem depicting the life of Gautama Buddha.
16. This appears however to be a conundrum not pondered in the Vedic world.

passages in the Vedic texts strongly suggestive of that claim, but these prove ultimately to be no more than a *façon de parler* not meant to be taken literally. As Shankaracharya[17] informs us: "*Ātman* (God conceived as the universal Witness) *is the only transmigrant.*" The point is that the *jiva*, in itself, has no being; as Christ declared to St. Catherine of Siena: "*I am He that is; you are she that is not.*" Immortality of any kind hinges thus upon a "union with God." And there appear to be precisely two options open in principle to mankind: the *nirvānic* and the Christian. And as we have noted, they differ to the point of being antipodal: in the Christian, namely, human nature survives and is in fact perfected, whereas in the Vedic it disappears—somewhat like a dewdrop "slipping into the shining sea."

One must of course be careful how one conceives of such "separation" between God and man as remains in the Christian Eschaton, a union which—from a Vedic point of vantage—seems to defy the distinction between the "real" and the "unreal," the "is" and "is not." What confronts us here, however, is not so much a logical conundrum as an inability to conceive of states which in truth exceed what we take to be the "human." The *nirvānic* state, on the other hand, is rendered comparatively unproblematic by the fact that its negation of the "human" is unqualified. It is the Christian Eschaton, thus, that proves to be profoundly enigmatic inasmuch as it envisages a survival of the human in a union with the Divine; and the most puzzling issue of all, it seems, centers upon what Christianity terms "*the resurrection*

---

17. One of the most revered sages of India: the Vedic Aquinas if you will, who also lived roughly around the same time.

of the body." You may recall how the erudite Athenians on the Areopagus took their leave the moment St. Paul broached that subject: "*some mocked, and others said, We will hear thee again on this matter.*"[18]

~

The Church has, as a rule, been focused upon the eschatological dichotomy of *heaven* and *hell*, to the exclusion of the Vedic Eschaton. The time is coming, however—and this, surely, relates to that prophesied "engagement with India"—when Catholic theologians will be confronted in earnest, and perhaps for the first time, by that *nirvānic* option; and as von Balthasar predicts, the resultant recognition may indeed prove to be of decisive significance to the Church. For it may provide access to what appears to have been, in truth, a *terra incognita* for theology. The fact is that Christ did not speak to us about the Vedic religion, which at the time had already flourished in India for centuries, and in the form of Buddhism had spread through much of Asia.[19]

It is finally to be noted that the categorical distinction between Salvation and the *nirvānic* option contradicts what Frithjof Schuon terms "the transcendent unity of religions," a position widely held nowadays in the most highly educated strata both in the East and in the West. This claim of "transcendent unity" reverses in a way the erstwhile stigma of "paganism": instead of reducing to demon worship, the Vedic religion has

18. Acts 17:32
19. I take it namely that Buddhism is inherently Vedic inasmuch as it aims at the same Eschaton, i.e., the *nirvānic*.

now supposedly swallowed up Christianity by reducing it to a kind of *bhakti* cult, of which the Vedic tradition already encompasses many![20]

The confusion is great, and it appears that a serious encounter between the Christian West and India may indeed be most timely: nothing less, perhaps, would suffice to clarify crucial issues, which for a very long time have been muddled on both sides. The prophesied East-West engagement may thus inaugurate a crucially significant understanding between the Christian and the Vedic religions; and who knows whether, in the providence of God, this might not open the door—for men and women the world over—to embrace the Salvation offered to mankind by Jesus Christ, which now at last they will recognize as the unique and incommensurable Gift it is.

II

By focusing upon the Vedic Eschaton and the means of its attainment—the *chittavrittinirodha*—to the exclusion virtually of all other elements—we have presented an exceedingly one-sided picture of the Vedic religion, our objective being to expose the chasm separating the Vedic and Christian eschatologies. Yet even though these respective "destinations" prove to be virtually antipodal, there exists nonetheless a profound kinship

---

20. The word *bhakti* means "love," which in this case is directed to various personifications of God widely revered in India, such as *Rāma* and *Krishna*. I think it is safe to opine that, judged from the highest level of Vedic doctrine, the *bhakti* cults can ultimately be no more than in some way preparatory to the supreme path: the one leading to the *nirvānic* option.

between Christianity and the Vedic religion, which we would like now to bring to light.

It needs, first of all, to be understood that the Vedic religion is not meant merely for the likes of a Ramana Maharshi, but has served as the spiritual compass and source of grace to the oldest extant civilization on Earth. It speaks in fact to every man, woman, and child born into the Vedic culture, and apparently not without success, seeing that the Vedic has to date vastly outlived every other religion. Despite the extreme esoterism surrounding its ultimate Eschaton and the Himalayan demands it places upon its monastic aspirants, it yet offers a spiritual path to those not called to the ascent of Mt. Everest. It does so, moreover, the one and only way this *can be* done: by way, namely, of *self-surrender to God in love and trust*. In fact, the vast majority of monks and laymen alike following the Vedic religion worship God in an inherently human form or guise—of which there are many—with the implicit understanding, it seems, that this "form" constitutes a concession to our human incapacity, acceptable to Almighty God. Let us be clear on this key issue: what is worshipped in the Vedic tradition is not the form, but what the form symbolizes or represents to him that worships—and I, for one, cannot doubt that this is indeed none other than God himself.

To be sure, this is not to deny the radical difference between the Vedic and the Christian worship, which is based—not upon a chosen form or *ishta devāta*[21]—but upon the Incarnation: upon the fact that

---

21. Not to be confused with the aforesaid *avātara*.

> *the Word was made flesh, and dwelt among us, (and we beheld his glory, the glory as of the only begotten of the Father) full of grace and truth!*[22]

It can thus be argued that there is actually no common measure between Vedic and Christian worship—and yet in a way *there is*, simply because God looks into the heart of whosoever approaches him with folded hands.

And let me add that the manifest depth, sincerity, and ardor of the Vedic worship I was privileged to witness during my travels—especially in the more remote and indigenous regions—have aroused my deepest admiration, and that in fact I returned to the West with a sense that the "Vedic India" I had experienced was in truth the most religious land I had ever known. Nowhere else had I encountered an entire populace so profoundly devoted to the practice of their religion!

In light of these reflections it may come as no surprise that the Vedic ethics proves to be in essence identical to the Christian. One could, of course, write a book on that subject alone; but perhaps a single reference may suffice to make this point clear. In answer to the question "what are the marks of perfection in the practice of *yoga*," Sri Krishna replies:

> *Him I hold to be the supreme yogi, O Arjuna, who looks on the pleasure and pain of all beings as he looks on them in himself.*[23]

---

22. John 1:14
23. Bhagavad Gītā 6:32

What indeed could be more quintessentially Christian than that! And I might note that in the course of my travels, I did on rare occasions encounter *sādhus* who seemed to exemplify this state—once in a Buddhist monastery near Kathmandu. These experiences stand out in my recollection as something not quite of this world.

Having alluded to the symbolic significance of the *gerua* color—the fact that it symbolizes an immolation—I would point out that the Vedic religion, in its ultimate manifestation, is based upon a sacrificial death. I find it immensely significant, however, that in this Vedic sacrifice the victim is apparently the human aspirant himself: does this not, in itself, proclaim the *nirvānic* nature of the corresponding Eschaton?

Contrast this now with the Sacrifice upon which Christianity is based, *the Death of Christ upon the Cross*: here it is the Incarnate God who offers Himself as the victim for the Salvation of humanity. It strikes me that this contrast proclaims both the kinship as well as the extreme disparity between the two religions: that although both are founded upon a Sacrificial Death, in the Vedic it is the *sādhu* who sacrifices himself for the attainment of the *nirvānic* Eschaton, whereas in the Christian it is Christ who offers Himself upon the Cross for all of mankind, *that we too may have eternal life*.[24] Incomprehensible as it may be, nothing less than this, it appears, can bestow upon us an immortality in which the human as such is not only preserved, but is

---

24. To be more accurate, one should however add that in Christianity, too, the human aspirant is called upon to undergo what might be termed a "death to himself."

in a sense *deified*. And nothing, too, can highlight as poignantly *the disparity between the two religions*, which may indeed be characterized as infinite.

III

So far we have neglected to take note of the fact that theology as such cannot but censure the very notion of what we have termed the *nirvānic* option. To the extent, namely, that it is based upon the premise of *creatio ex nihilo* as this tenet is generally understood,[25] it is bound to attribute a *being* to the cosmos which, in the final count, the cosmos does not possess. This failing or imperfection is to be recognized as a necessary consequence of the requirement that theology *per se* be comprehensible to mankind at large. After all: if it takes years of study to make, say, a rocket engineer, one need hardly be surprised if not everyone is capable of grasping the mysteries of God!

The fact is that there exists a kind of "common sense" ontology based upon the ordinary notion of "things," and that the public at large is more or less restricted to that level of comprehension. The circumstance, clearly, that theology is addressed to that very "public at large"—that it is thus "catechetical" or "exoteric"—entails that very limitation. But let us not fail to note that a "things" ontology as such excludes the Vedic Eschaton categorically, for it negates the pivotal premise that is *"truly*

---

25. It is to be noted that there are versions of the *creatio ex nihilo*—for instance, St. Augustine's interpretation—which do not thus hypostatize cosmic reality. There has however been a tendency in post-Patristic times to understand this concept in inherently fundamentalist terms.

perceived by the seers of Truth": the ontological fact, namely, that "*the unreal never is.*" The same applies evidently to corresponding tenets of Christian doctrine as well, beginning with the "*ego sum qui sum*" of Exodus 3:14, which in fact is ontologically commensurate with the Vedic "*never is.*"

In short, *exoteric or* "*catechetical*" *teaching does not suffice* for a comprehension of either religion. And this entails, in particular, that *theology alone does not suffice* for the comprehension of Christianity: a touch, at least, of esoterism is ultimately needed as well. The problem resides in the theological notion of *creatio ex nihilo* inasmuch as it attributes a *being* to the cosmos which, *in fine finali*, the cosmos does not possess. No one, however, need be surprised that an ontology comprehensible, say, to a high school student should prove not to be the last word!

The integral tradition of Christianity compensates for the aforesaid limitation by the fact that *creatio ex nihilo* theology does not stand alone—as perhaps some theologians are tempted to think—but is *de jure* complemented by a higher teaching, which in former times was termed *esoteric* as distinguished from *exoteric*, and likewise *oral* as opposed to *written* or *catechetical*. St. Paul informs us of this noetic dichotomy in unmistakable terms when he declares:

> *And I, brethren, could not speak unto you as unto spiritual, but as unto carnal, even as unto babes in Christ. I have fed you with milk, and not with meat: for hitherto you were not able to bear it, neither yet now are ye able.*[26]

---

26. 1 Cor. 3:1-2

Yet, even so, "meat" was by no means lacking in the early Church. Consider, for example, what St. Gregory of Nyssa discloses on the subject of creation, which in fact is fully concordant with the Vedic ontology:

> *It seems to me that at the time the great Moses was instructed in the theophany he came to know that none of those things which are apprehended by sense perception and contemplated by the understanding really subsists, but that the transcendent essence and cause of the universe, on which everything depends, alone subsists.*[27]

It needs hardly to be pointed out that this does not square with latter-day *creatio ex nihilo* theology. The same unquestionably *esoteric* point, moreover, is made—and perhaps even more decisively—by St. Augustine, a Doctor of the Church no less. Addressing himself to God, he writes:

> *I beheld these others beneath thee, and saw that they neither altogether are, nor altogether are not. An existence they have, because they are from thee; and yet no existence, because they are not what thou art. For only that really is, that remains unchangeably.*[28]

---

27. *The Life of Moses*, II, 24.
28. *Confessions*, VII, 11. This comes very close to the Vedic text we have quoted: "*The unreal never is. The Real never ceases to be.*" Even the third part—"*This fact is clearly perceived by the seers of Truth*"—has its counterpart in the Augustinian "*I beheld.*" As regards St. Augustine's assertion that "*only that really is, that remains unchangeably,*" let us note that this is inherently Platonist, and accords with what we have termed the "tripartite cosmology." See, for instance, *The Vertical Ascent* (Philos-Sophia Initiative Foundation, 2021), the first section of chapter 2.

Now, this strikes me as the quintessential recognition definitive of esoteric ontology as such. And let us not fail to note that it categorically undercuts the fundamentalist *creatio ex nihilo* by reducing created entities to a manifestation of something they are not, and thus implicates an "ontology of misperception" reminiscent, at least, of the Hindu *māyā*. On this absolutely fundamental issue St. Augustine appears to be in basic agreement with the sages of India.

Getting back to von Balthasar's prophecy: might it not be a providential function of that "engagement with India" to enable the authentically "esoteric" to course once again freely in the bloodstream of the Church, as it did in the days of St. Gregory and St. Augustine? And might this not be what is ultimately called for to reverse the latter-day decline?

∼

It may be of interest to reflect upon Jean Borella's claim that "there exists a way of *gnosis*—properly so called—within the bosom of Christianity."[29] By "*gnosis properly so called*" Borella means a direct knowledge or *vision* of God, such as Christ promises to the "*pure of heart*."[30] The first and most crucial observation to be made in that regard is that the subject of that *seeing* is unquestionably *man* himself: it is "*they*"—the "*pure of heart*"

---

29. *The Secret of the Christian Way* (SUNY Press, 2001), p. 5. Let me add that I regard Jean Borella as perhaps the deepest and best-informed Catholic theologian of our day; we will have occasion to discuss his views in the final chapter.

30. Matt. 5:8

themselves—that shall "*see God*"! This *vision of God* is consequently *not* of the *nirvānic* kind.

I propose to show that such a "*way of gnosis*" is in fact documented in the writings of Meister Eckhart, the renowned Dominican who has been the subject of speculation and controversy for a good 700 years. To which I might add that I empathize with those who perceive Eckhart as a master "from whom God hid nothing": the more deeply one probes his writings, the less preposterous this claim appears.

By that very token, however, his teaching proves to be incurably esoteric: dangerously so, in fact. There is actually good reason why the Inquisitors condemned 28 of Eckhart's propositions as "evil seed" and "thorns of error":[31] that is what they may well be for those who cannot rightly understand what in truth Eckhart affirms. The fact, moreover, that the Inquisitors themselves may not have had the foggiest idea what the Meister is actually talking about does not matter in the least: what counts is that they picked up what lesser minds might glean from his discourse. On the other hand, there are seekers who may indeed discover in these proscribed treatises that "*way of gnosis*" concealed "*within the bosom of Christianity.*"

Before we turn to the relevant texts, a comment may be in order. Contrary to the customary characterization of Eckhart as a so-called "mystic," it is namely to be understood that he did not abandon the Scholastic method, of which he was a consummate master, but that, on the contrary, he pursued that method to its very end.

---

31. *In agro dominico*, promulgated in 1329 (two years, happily, after the Meister's death).

And certainly one may wonder why his illustrious predecessor seems not so much as touch upon the esoteric side of the Scholastic quest—except in what appears to be his last didactic utterance, addressed to his faithful secretary Reginald. Here, near the end of his life, St. Thomas differentiates categorically between the *esoteric* and the *exoteric* realms, and specifies their respective ranks. "I now *see*," he begins—which, at least in retrospect, identifies the statement as esoteric[32]—"that all I have *written*"—a reference evidently to the exoteric or catechetical—"is mere straw": "*mihi videtur ut palea.*" But alas: it appears that this magisterial and singularly enlightening declaration—remarkable both for its content and its apodictic brevity—has as a rule been roundly ignored by the Thomistic community.

The task of pursuing the Scholastic ascent to the very summit has thus apparently fallen to the Meister from whom, reputedly, "God hid nothing."

Let us then turn to Matthew 5:8: "*Blessed are the pure in heart: for they shall see God.*" It behooves us now to reflect upon that "*purity of heart*": for it need hardly be pointed out that our customary understanding of "purity"—which might be characterized broadly as "moral"—does not suffice. What stands in question might rather be termed an "ontological" kind of purity, which is something else entirely; and it appears that

---

32. The point is that the esoteric stands to the exoteric as vision stands to inference. The esoteric is thus comparable to a knowing "*face to face*" as opposed to "*through a glass, darkly.*"

Meister Eckhart may stand alone—at least in the Christian world—in his conception of what in truth this entails.

The crucial text pertains to a German sermon[33] addressed to women religious and laity, based upon John 16:16, the fragment: "*A little while, and ye shall not see me: and again, a little while and ye shall see me.*" Breaking all precedent, Eckhart renders the Vulgate "*modicum*"—not as "a little while"—but simply as "a little something," whatever it may be. And this leads him to conclude that "*However small a thing it is which sticks to the soul, we shall not see God.*"

By this singular masterstroke, Eckhart has opened the door to an inquiry into what may properly be called *Christian yoga*: an inherently Christian version of the *chittavrittinirodha* no less. What is it, then, that differentiates this Christian yoga from the Vedic? It evidently cannot but reside in the *identity of the yogi* himself. We must remember that, in the *modicum* text, Christ is addressing his most intimate disciples at the Last Supper: His very own *Apostles* no less!

Christian yoga differs, thus, from the Vedic—not in the *chittavrittinirodha* as such, which is simply what the words declare it to be—but by the fact that the Christian yogi is intimately united with Christ. It is by way of that union that he is able not only to accomplish the *nirodha*, but to *survive* it so as to "*see God*" whom "*no man hath seen at any time.*"[34] As Christ Himself explains:

33. Sermon 69
34. John 1:18

> *And this is life eternal, that they might know thee the only true God, and Jesus Christ, whom thou hast sent.*[35]

~

Everything hinges upon Eckhart's interpretation of the *modicum* text: the fact that the *nirodha* of the last *chittavritti*—the last "impurity" that "sticks to the soul"—results instantly in the vision of God. I wish now to point out that Eckhart arrives at that interpretation by way of an argument which—besides being at once esoteric and solidly scriptural—proves to be quintessentially Trinitarian.

The argument traces back to Eckhart's *Expositio Libri Genesis*, the first of his two commentaries on Genesis, to the following passage namely:

> In one and the same *nunc stans* in which He was God and in which He begot His coeternal Son as God equal to Himself in all things, He also created the world: "*God spoke once and for all*" (Job 22:14). He speaks in begetting the Son because the Son is the Word; He speaks in creating creatures, "*He spoke and they were made, He commanded and they were created*" (Ps. 32:9). This is why it says in another Psalm, "*God has spoken once and for all and I have heard two things*" (Ps. 61:12). The "two things" are heaven and earth, or rather "these two," that is, the emanation of the Persons and the creation of the world, but "He speaks"

---

35. John 17:3

them both "once and for all"; "*He has spoken once and for all.*"[36]

The question, of course, is how one and the same divine "command" can give rise to two such utterly disparate effects; and Eckhart's answer is that "the emanation of the Persons" and "the creation of the world" *are not* in truth "*two things.*"

We are plunged thus—at a single stroke—into the most radical esoterism, a Christian version, in fact, of the Vedantic *advaita*:[37] the claim, namely, that "the second thing" we have "heard" is not a separate reality at all. What is it, then, that "second thing"? Eckhart calls it a "*modicum*," by which he means something that "sticks to the soul." What needs to be grasped is that such a *modicum* is not a reality in itself, but something, rather, which derives such seeming reality as it has from the fact that it is *seen* or conceived. It is thus a *chittavritti*, which as such is subject in principle to the yogic *nirodha*, or uprooting. The crucial point is that this *modicum*—and hence the intentional "world" at large—proves not to be a "second thing" for the reason that "*God has spoken once and for all.*" In Christian metaphysics no less than in the Vedic, the last word turns out to be "nonduality" or *advaita*.

This nonduality brings us back to St. Gregory's "*transcendent essence*" which "*alone subsists,*" while "*these*

---

36. Quoted in B. M. McGinn, *Meister Eckhart: Teacher and Preacher* (Paulist Press, 1986), pp. 84-5.

37. The Sanskrit term means literally "nonduality": the nonduality of God, the supreme Reality, and the cosmos. The difference is not a matter of *being*, but of *knowing*: "*God has spoken once and for all, but I have heard two things.*"

others"—which comprise what we deem to be the universe—"*have no existence*" as St. Augustine avers, "*because they are not what thou art.*" Like it or not—concur with it or not—this verdict conforms to the ultimate esoterism, both Vedic and Christian. In a word, our present or "normal" mode of seeing is fundamentally flawed: the fact is that we perceive as *entities* things that have no being of their own, things which actually reduce to a mere Eckhartian *modicum*. The "purity of heart" Christ enjoins upon us to cultivate must therefore entail the elimination of these *modicums*, a purification which in the end brings us *face to face* with God the Father through God the Son, who is in truth the Word "*spoken once and for all.*"

I say "us" referring to a Christian united to the Incarnate Word: it is this union, I say, that differentiates Christian yoga from the Vedic. It is this union with the Incarnate Word that enables the Christian yogi to "survive" the *nirodha* so as to "see" God. Does this mean that, in the Vedic scenario, there is no "survivor" at all? I did not say that; and in fact, one can't. Vedanta teaches that the *ātman*—what it views as the true Self—remains; and most certainly we do not deny this. What presently concerns us, however, is the fact that our "human self" does *not* survive.

⁂

Eckhart broaches the subject of Christian yoga in his Latin Sermon XLIX based upon Matthew 22:20, the words: "*Whose are this image and inscription?*" What apparently fascinates him is the fact that there are two kinds of "image": the kind that is separated from its exemplar—like the image of Caesar upon a Roman coin, which is what one terms a *form*—and the kind that is not separated therefrom. He goes on, moreover, to affirm that only the latter kind is truly an image, because "*image as such cannot be separated from that of which it is an image.*" And he concludes with the observation that "*image is the principle of form.*" Having thus distinguished ontologically between *image* and *form*, Eckhart seeks to comprehend the distinction between "*the two things I have heard*": the emanation of the Persons and the creation of the world.

The decisive step is epistemological: how do we know a so-called external entity, say a stone? We know it, Eckhart avers, by means of an intermediary element or *medium*, and conceivably by an entire sequence of such *media*. The *media* by which "the ten thousand things" of this world are known prove therefore to be the *modicums* that "stick to the soul" and prevent us from seeing the Word. There must however be something—on pain of infinite regress—that is seen directly, *without a medium*. And that is what Eckhart refers to as the *vünkelin* or "little spark," and affirms to be inseparable from the Word: "*so completely one and joined together that one cannot comprehend any distinction between them.*"[38] The point is that *the identity or oneness of the Word and the vünkelin entails the nonduality of "the two things I have heard.*" What Eckhart gives us is in essence *a Trinitarian ontology of the cosmos itself*, a *reductio* of "the second thing I have heard" to the first.[39]

---

38. Quoted in B. M. McGinn, op. cit., p. 314.
39. For an in-depth treatment of this question I refer to *Christian Gnosis: From Saint Paul to Meister Eckhart* (Angelico Press, 2008), the chapter entitled "Meister Eckhart on Creation."

No wonder the Eckhartian doctrine is esoteric in the extreme! And how could it *not* be seen as "heretical" by the Inquisitors—in the wake of the Fourth Lateran Council, no less, which seems to perceive *creation* as an inherently *temporal* act. On the other hand, if even the integral cosmos itself transcends the bound of time—as is not only the consensus of the great philosophical traditions, but can be argued even on scientific grounds[40]—what to speak of the creative Act!

One final point needs to be explicated. It may seem, namely, that the completion of the *chittavrittinirodha* as such suffices to bring about the consummation of the Christian Way—which would eliminate the fundamental distinction we have drawn between the Vedic and the Christian Eschaton: between the *nirvānic* option and the Salvation offered to mankind by Christ. Yet as previously noted, what distinguishes Christian from Vedic yoga categorically is the nature of the yogi himself: the fact that the Christian has already entered into a certain union with Christ. *It is in a way Christ who "does the yoga"; and one might say that as the "illusory" self of the human subject—tied to "mental modifications" or modicums—disappears, his true human self, rendered such by an inseparable union with Christ, remains as the subject of the Beatific Vision.*

∽

Meister Eckhart's recognition that authentic *gnosis* demands the *chittavrittinirodha*—the "uprooting" of all "mental modifications"—reveals a truth almost

---

40. See *The Vertical Ascent*, op. cit., ch. 2.

universally unrecognized in the Western world: the fact, namely, that *authentic gnosis* or *Knowledge of God transcends the conceptual order of knowing*. And this entails that *gnosis*, properly so called, *transcends not only the order of theology, but that of esoterism as well*. In the final count it does not suffice "to think correctly": *it is ultimately needful to stop "thinking" at all*. It appears that the *sādhu* who confided to me that "*we are seeking to enter the abode of death*" knew, after all, what he was saying. Whether it be the Vedic or the Christian path: a "death" must invariably precede the attainment of immortality, whichever of the two kinds it may be.

Ours is indeed a knowing "*through a glass, darkly*" as distinguished from "*face to face*"[41] which alone constitutes *gnosis*, properly so called. The fact is that *conceptual* knowing—however marvelous and even *supernatural* it may be—does not take us all the way, but needs at last to be superseded. Authentic esoterism, though it may indeed apprise us of this fact, is yet incapable of bestowing the *gnosis* to which it alludes.

This recognition is needed, in the first place, to forestall an overvaluation of the esoteric: its elevation to the status of an ultimate truth, when in fact it can be no more than "a finger pointing to the moon." We need to realize that the *chittavrittinirodha* is not simply a Vedic thing, but proves to be a *sine qua non* for any authentic knowing of God, which simply cannot be attained on a "mental" plane. Remember: "*however small a thing it is which sticks to the soul, we shall not see God.*" And let us not fail to note that this recognition gives to the Christic "*purity of heart*" an altogether new sense, which radically transcends the moral order: what stands at issue is

41. 1 Cor. 13:12

nothing less than *the central mystery of yoga*, be it Vedic or Christian. *Gnosis* and the yogic *nirodha* are therefore commensurate; the only distinction to be made is between Vedic and Christian *gnosis*.

∼

Doctrinal formulations—from the simplest catechism to the most sublime esoteric doctrine—have of course not only their place, but their necessity; yet even so, *as a statement of ultimate truth they invariably fall short of the mark*. Christ Himself apprises us of this fact when He declares: "*I have yet many things to say unto you, but ye cannot bear them now.*"[42] It needs namely to be understood that these "*many things*" are not to be conceived as so many "additional" teachings—a matter of increasing the breadth or range of our knowledge—but refer rather to the dimension of *depth*. What stands at issue is that supreme Truth, alluded to by Christ when He declared: "*Ye shall know the truth, and the truth shall make you free.*" The decisive point is that this truth *is not attainable on a mental plane*, but calls for that consummate "*purity of heart*" which is not moral but substantive or ontological, and which few in this life attain. Rare indeed is a St. Augustine, or a Meister Eckhart!

IV

Finally, having earlier acknowledged the central role—in both the Christian and the Vedic spheres—of "*self-surrender to God in love and trust*," let us note

---

42. John 16:12

emphatically that there is absolutely nothing "exoteric," or in any way deceptive in that at all, which is to say that *there is no "ontology"—no theorizing of any kind—in love*. The child loves its mother no less on account of its inability to know who in truth she is, or where she comes from. And as a matter of fact, within the profane civilization of our time, it is typically the simple and childlike who are most apt to ascend the spiritual ladder all the way to the heights of sainthood. If one should ask, moreover, how it is possible to be united to God in such seeming ignorance, the reason may well be that—in its innermost essence—*love is itself something divine*. As the Beloved Disciple informs us: "*Deus caritas est.*"[43]

So long, therefore, as it is pervaded by the love of God, even the humblest "*following of Christ*" can lead to full and perfect sanctity, along with the fruits thereof—which, I surmise, include a wisdom deeper in its simplicity than the most perspicacious speculations of the erudite. The simple fact is that *God loves his own*.

---

43. "*God is love*" (1 John 4:16).

2

FROM BENEDICTINE TO *SĀDHU*: THE CASE OF HENRI LE SAUX

HENRI LE SAUX WAS BORN in 1910 in Brittany, sent to the Petit Séminaire de Chateaugiron in 1921, and entered the Benedictine monastery at Kergonan in 1929. "Of course it needs guts to become a holy monk" he writes soon after entering,

> but despite its difficulty, I feel one is bound to aim high. A monk cannot accept mediocrity, only extremes are appropriate for him. The richness of the monastic life I have only begun to glimpse now that I have entered it for good; and I still feel myself as if inundated, dazzled by it; it is too vast for one to be able to grasp it all at once.[1]

Little did he know how very true these words would prove to be! And I would add that the step was difficult for his family as well, especially his mother. "You are going to pray so much for us, my little one," she writes

---

1. Quoted in Shirley du Boulay, *The Cave of the Heart* (Orbis Books, 2005), p. 17. Unless otherwise specified, biographical references are to this source.

to him, "that God will certainly send me the courage to endure such a trial… I believe, my Henry, that I love you even more than before" (20).[2]

Six years after entering the monastery, Henri Le Saux was ordained, and by all indications seemed destined to spend the remainder of his life as a Benedictine monk. Yet one can see in retrospect that there were depths in his soul to which he had not yet fully awakened, that would in time lead him to strike out into a very different world, there to pursue what in the end he came to perceive as his true vocation.

An early sign of these as yet hidden vistas appeared a year before his ordination in the form of a passionate desire to visit India; yet for about a decade he confided this aspiration to no one. At last he shared his "dreams of India," first with his sister, and finally with his fellow monks. It turns out that his feelings regarding the monastery at Kergonan were mixed: that he loved it in many ways and held a deep affection for his monastic brethren stands above doubt; yet it appears that there were within him contrary voices as well. As Shirley du Boulay, his biographer, informs us:

> On the other hand, there were times when the negative side could not be contained and he admitted to a distaste for the monastery and to a disenchantment with the church, conceding that life in the monastery did not fulfill him, indeed that "it was in my deep dissatisfaction that my desire to come to India was born." (41)

---

2. The numbers in parentheses refer to pages in Shirley du Boulay's book.

And she goes on to observe—very perspicaciously—that "how he developed such an overwhelming desire to go to India may not be clear, but the strength of his longing to go there was not in doubt. It was as strong as—arguably stronger than—his initial vocation to the monastic life." And certainly the remainder of his story amply confirms this surmise.

As might however be expected, when Henri finally approached the abbot of the Kergonan monastery, the latter proved not to be overjoyed. After Fr. Le Saux had conveyed his aspiration to his superior he was treated to "a lovely homily telling me that I had entered the monastic life to sanctify myself and that it was no good dreaming of going far away, that by living the monastic life here I would be doing just as much for India, and so on and so forth…" (46): how very true—and yet how utterly beside the point!

～

Let this suffice by way of introduction to this highly unusual monastic: this "Christian *sādhu*" if you will. Needless to say, Henri Le Saux did eventually succeed in persuading his abbot to let him go; and on August 14, 1948, he arrived finally at Colombo:

> I was glued to the ship's rail; people tried to talk to me, but I could only answer with difficulty. I had been waiting for this moment for fifteen years. (53)

Surely the future Swami Abhishiktananda must have foreknown, in the depths of his being, that an altogether new life—and in fact, a new religion as well—awaited him.

Readers interested in pursuing the story of this unique "man of God" are well advised to read the excellent account given by Shirley du Boulay; for us it will suffice to touch upon the events most pivotal to the formation of his subsequent outlook. And it stands beyond doubt that the single most decisive encounter—which seems in fact to have "sealed" Henri Le Saux's fate then and there—was his meeting with the great Ramana Maharshi, the sage already mentioned in chapter 1.

In point of fact, Fr. Le Saux visited the Maharshi twice, soon after his arrival in India. Sri Ramana resided at the time in an *āshram* built by his devotees within the shadow of Arunachala, the mountain on which he had spent a good part of his life living in a cave. Jules Monchanin—a friend of Fr. Le Saux who was himself a priest, a monk, and a hermit—took his comrade to see the Maharshi, with the significant comment that there "is not an *atom* of Christianity in that serene and beautiful face" (67); but apparently this exceedingly pertinent observation did not impact his companion.

No one need be surprised that the Benedictine who had been dreaming of "India" half his life should fall under the spiritual influence of the Hindu giant. As Arthur Osborne—a British author who himself became a follower—observed:

> Sri Bhagavan would turn to the devotee, his eyes fixed upon him with blazing intentness. The luminosity, the power of his eyes, pierced into one,

breaking down the thought-process. Sometime it was as though an electric current was passing though one, a vast peace, a flood of light. As one devotee has described it: "Suddenly Bhagavan turned his luminous, transparent eyes on me. Before that I could not stand his gaze for long. Now I looked straight back into those terrible, wonderful eyes, how long I could not tell. They held me in a kind of vibration distinctly audible to me." (67)

As it turns out, Fr. Le Saux's reaction to the Maharshi at his first face-to-face encounter was somewhat mixed. Yet, by the time of his second—and last—visit, such was no longer the case; here is how he describes his final impression:

> The invisible halo of the Sage had been perceived by something in me deeper than any words. Unknown harmonics awoke in my heart. A melody made itself felt, and especially an all-embracing ground-bass... In the Sage of Arunachala of our own time I discerned the unique Sage of the eternal India, the unbroken succession of her sages, her ascetics, her seers; it was as if the very soul of India penetrated to the very depths of my own soul and held mysterious communion with it. It was a call that pieced through everything, tore it apart and opened a mighty abyss. (72)

As his biographer aptly observes: he "realized the depth within himself to which the Sage of Arunachala had pierced. He would never be quite the same again."

∼

Two and a half years later Fr. Le Saux returned to Tiruvannamalai. By this time the Maharshi had left this world, and the center of attraction had begun to shift from the *āshram*, where the Maharshi had resided, to the adjacent mountain, which our Benedictine came to experience more and more imperiously as the source of the power drawing a multitude of *sādhus* and pilgrims of every description to the site in ever greater numbers. As Shirley du Boulay observes: "The mountain had begun to cast its spell over him" (73); and as a matter of fact, Fr. Le Saux tells us so himself in words resonant with inspiration:

> It is all up with anyone who has paused, even for a moment, to attend to the gentle whisper of Arunachala. Arunachala has already taken him captive, and will play with him without mercy to the bitter end. Darkness after light, desertion after embraces, he will never let him go until he has emptied him of everything in himself that is not the one and only Arunachala and that still persists in giving him a name, as one names *another*—until he has been finally swallowed up, having disappeared for ever in the shining of his Dawn-light, *Aruna*. (73)

"So at the end of March 1952," Ms. du Boulay informs us, "Dom Henri Le Saux, a European Benedictine monk in his early forties, having by then taken the name of Swami Abhishiktananda, for the first time dressed, ate, and lived as a *sādhu*, a wandering monk, in the caves of Arunachala" (74).

"His day started early in the morning," she continues. "While it was still dark, he would say Mass in his cave, deep in the heart of the mountain. Then he would sit in his *sacro speco* ('sacred space' as St. Benedict's cave at Subiaco was known) and wait for the Sun to rise." And on the very first evening in this *sacro speco*, Abhishiktananda resolved that he would live the rest of his life as a *sannyāsi*, a Hindu—or Hindu-Christian—monastic.

At this time he remained in that cave for ten days, observing complete silence, following which he had to leave. He returned to that Arunachala cave the same year for three weeks, and then moved to another, known among *sādhus* as "the spring of the milk of grace." He became accustomed thus to live in solitude, "willing to remain forever in my cave, keeping silence, without any concern for keeping witness, to be the first Christian for God at the Holy Mountain of Arunachala." He speaks in rapturous tones of "the abstinence from all thought, of the indescribable solitude of the Alone, deep within." How beautifully his biographer has put it: "Silence was to be the vast arena in which the drama of his search was to be played out" (76).

∽

In course of time, however, something unexpected came secretly to pass: the Vedic religion—in the form of *advaita* or "nondualist" Vedanta—came in effect to replace Christianity. To be sure, this is doubtless the last thing Fr. Le Saux had consciously intended when he set his sights upon India. It is in fact clear from early references that it was his intention—like that of every Catholic missionary—to bring the light of Christ to the Hindus, to whom he had even referred as *païens*: as "pagans" no less.

Slowly however—yet inexorably, it seems—Vedic India worked its magic upon the French Benedictine. And whereas his friend, Fr. Jules Monchanin refused to be thus affected, and for the most part kept a safe distance from the sacred Hindu sites—from Arunachala and its caves for instance—Fr. Henri Le Saux plunged in without fear or reservations, eager to savor the sacred springs of the *sanātana dharma*, the "eternal religion" as the Hindus refer to their own. And by all indications, this proved to be indeed the "draught of immortality" for which he pined in the very core of his being: a potion which apparently was destined to terminate his mortal existence.

We are not suggesting, of course, that this transition from Benedictine monk to Vedantic *sādhu* took place instantly, or without travail. The biography chronicles the years of transition: the doubts, conflicts, and indeed agonies through which he passed. It recalls a time, for example, when the Vedantic *sādhu*-to-be avers that it was his "long acquaintance with the liturgy and the early fathers that 'saves me' from Shankara's *advaita*" (105). The fact remains, however, that "Shankara's *advaita*" did triumph in the end.

The decisive driving force in this transformation, it seems, was not primarily doctrinal, but derives rather from direct spiritual experience attendant upon intensive yogic practice. Abhishiktananda tells us so himself in the clearest terms when he speaks of "having found in *advaita* a peace and a bliss never experienced before," while in the same breath he admits to a "dread that perhaps, most probably, all that my latent Christianity suggests to me is nonetheless true, and that therefore *advaita* must be sacrificed to it" (106). He even goes on to agonize that "in committing myself totally to *advaita*, if Christianity is true, I risk committing myself to a false path for eternity." Yet in the end, the "peace and bliss never experienced before" prevailed evidently over all his doubts and tribulations. And let us not fail to note what is perhaps the most significant point of all: the fact that Fr. Le Saux speaks of his "*latent* Christianity." For what else can that adjective signify than that his Christianity *was no longer practiced, no longer effectively believed*! It appears that, at this point, the die had already been cast.

It is to be noted that amid all the fluctuations and soul-searching through which Henri Le Saux passed, the one theoretical possibility which appears never to have occurred to him is that *Christianity and Vedanta may both be true, but lead to different Ends*: the former to Salvation, the latter to the *nirvānic* Eschaton. He seemed rather to presume from the outset that there can only be one ultimate End—one universal Eschaton—open to mankind, a premise which, in a way, sealed his destiny. Following his fateful encounter with Ramana Maharshi, namely, there could be no more doubt regarding the reality of the Vedic Eschaton: he had *seen* its very embodiment in that "serene and beautiful face" in which "there is not an *atom* of Christianity" as Fr. Monchanin had astutely observed.

There can be little doubt that it was the direct spiritual impact of the fully enlightened Sage that, in the end, proved irresistible; and it appears that Fr. Le Saux realized this instantly. As he tells us himself: "It was as if the very soul of India penetrated to the very depth of my own soul and held mysterious communion… It was a call that pierced through everything, tore it apart and opened a mighty abyss." One may surmise that, at this very moment, his fate was sealed.

∼

Let us ponder the postulate of "one absolute and ultimate Eschaton" which Abhishiktananda appeared to accept without question following his encounter with the Maharshi, if not before. To begin with, I would point out that this places Christianity at a great disadvantage vis-à-vis the Vedanta: for if the Christian Eschaton is indeed the veritable "antipode" of the Vedic—as we have argued in chapter 1—it is hardly surprising that such Christian practices as Abhishiktananda may have tried to integrate into his yogic discipline did not have the desired effect! It appears, moreover, that Abhishiktananda himself was by no means unaware of this incongruity, and that the more fully Vedantic he became in his overall formation, the more decisively he took sides. In a letter to a priest friend, for example, he freely admits to the ongoing transformation:

> From long habit I was extremely attached to the Liturgy; on Easter morning, I insist on reciting Matins and Lauds in spite of the non-obligation; however the Liturgy meant nothing to me any more… The Psalms are so exterior, so *māyā* as they say in India. I would have liked my Holy Week better in solitude… In the Eternal, what is the celebration of Time? How artificial, it seems, to give life to a particular day in

time, which is "consumed" in the eternity through which we pass. (107)

What Abhishiktananda evidently fails to grasp is that *Christianity does not reduce to Vedanta*, and that the Salvation it offers to mankind differs categorically from the Vedantic *nirvāna*. His lament itself corroborates this contention: the reason the Psalms, for instance, strike him as "so exterior" is that the "Hinduized" Benedictine himself has become "exterior"—not only to Christianity—but to the Judeo-Christian tradition at large. As we have argued in chapter 1—and regardless of what the aficionados of "transcendent unity" may say—*Vedanta and Christianity are in truth as different as night and day.*

The discrepancy between the two religions—the two "ways"—could not in fact be more extreme: on the one hand the notion that the *summum bonum* of human existence consists in a return to its primary Source, and on the other the promise of an End for the sake of which the person was brought into such being as he presently owns. The only way, therefore, these two options can coincide is if the last End of the Christian religion proves to be identical to the primary Source.

If I may be pardoned a "human, all too human" response, which can do no more than identify me as belonging to the Judeo-Christian branch of humanity: the notion of an exodus for the sake of a return to the starting point—an exodus which entails incalculable risks and agonies—this strikes me as the supreme absurdity: the most flagrant example conceivable of "*a tale told by an idiot, full of sound and fury, signifying nothing.*" In my own life, at any rate, it was this recognition that at last opened the door to my conversion—or better said, reconversion—to Christianity. It was indeed *"the Good News"* of Salvation that I now embraced with all the more gladness and gratitude for having been deprived of this incomparable Promise for such a long time. The attraction of the *advaitic* Eschaton, which did cast its spell over me when I sojourned in the Himalayan regions—be it among *sādhus* or alone—seemed now to have lost its erstwhile power to attract and inspire. As Christ declares: no man *"can serve two masters"*; and by now, mine had become clearly manifest.

∼

Getting back to Swami Abhishiktananda: in his case there can hardly be the slightest doubt that the Vedic option fulfilled the deepest aspirations of his soul to perfection. Remember his words: *"It was a call that pierced through everything, tore it apart and opened a mighty abyss."* Following a transitional period, during which Christianity had still a certain residual claim upon his soul, the final transition—from Benedictine monk to Vedantic *sādhu*—appears in the end to have been consummated. The salient point I wish to make is that, to understand aright what Abhishiktananda has to say following that final conversion, we need to bear in mind that what henceforth confronts us is no longer a Christian, but a spiritually advanced *sādhu* who sees the world through Vedantic eyes. Let no one be misled, let no one be bewildered: the voice you hear is no longer Christian, but fully Vedantic. Take for instance the following passage:

> Christ is the essential intermediary between the Father and myself. But an intermediary who does not cause any separation. For he is at once identical with me and identical with the Father. I say "I" only in him, and he says "I" only in the Father. And the mystery of the Spirit is all-pervasive... In my return to my origin, there is a stage in which my consciousness, in its movement towards definitive *advaita*, passes through the condition of Christ's consciousness, having in truth become Christ, as St. Paul said. (112)

What in the world is one to make of this?

From a Christian point of vantage the statement bristles obviously with absurdities—not to speak of blatant heresies, such as "having in truth become Christ"! But as I say: we must bear in mind that Abhishiktananda speaks no longer as a Christian, but as the Vedantist he has become. And from a Vedantic point of vantage, what he says does make sense—which is hardly surprising if one recalls that, in this optic, all things eventually merge as one moves towards the ultimate Source. So far from being heretical—not to say blasphemous—the notion that "in my return to my origin" this man, Henri Le Saux, should in a sense "become Christ" is utterly unremarkable, given that it is ultimately implied by the Vedantic *advaita*, its categorical *nondualism*.

What, on the other hand, I do find remarkable is that it seems never to have occurred to our Benedictine *sādhu* that, from a Vedantic point of view, *one cannot comprehend the first thing about Christianity.*

It may moreover come as a surprise to many that this verdict is in fact consistent with the Vedic wisdom itself: it happens namely that the Vedic tradition as such *does not* perceive the Vedanta as "the one and only ultimate truth"! That immemorial teaching is thus incomparably wiser than the Western converts who—almost to a man—do conceive of Vedanta in precisely these superlative terms.

According to the Vedic tradition, there are fundamentally six ways of viewing the world—misleadingly referred to as "the six systems of Indian philosophy" by Max Müller *et al.*—corresponding in fact to the six directions of space. And whereas Vedanta is indeed regarded as the highest of the six—inasmuch as it corresponds to the vertically "upward" direction—it is by no means conceived as the "absolute" Abhishiktananda takes it to be. What needs to be grasped is that, where the West speaks of "philosophy," the Vedic tradition itself speaks of *darśana*: what might almost be termed a "point of view." There is in this a recognition of the fact that "what you see" depends upon "the direction" in which you "look," and that there are basically six options. And this means that whereas *advaita* Vedanta may indeed be the "highest" of the six *darśanas*, it is yet but a *darśana* itself.

My point, then, is that *advaita* Vedanta, *traditionally conceived*, is by no means the absolute Western pundits and converts generally take it to be. Admittedly, it is the *darśana* adopted by *sādhus* in quest of the *nirvānic* Eschaton: with the clear understanding, however, that in the realization of that Eschaton all human conceptions—including that of "*advaita* Vedanta" itself—are instantly transcended. And this should come as no surprise: after all, it hardly requires metaphysical genius to see that doctrinal Vedanta itself does not survive the yogic *nirodha*, and is in fact negated from the start by the Upanishadic "*neti, neti*"—the ubiquitous "not so, not so."

The vital point concerning the teaching of Christianity, on the other hand, is the fact that it does *not* in truth reduce to a *darśana*: that, *being founded by the Incarnate Word*, it stands *above* all *darśanas*, inclusive of *advaita* Vedanta itself. As Jesus Christ declares: "*the words that I speak unto you, they are spirit, and they are life.*" It follows that, *to interpret the teachings of Christ in Vedantic terms, is to deprive them of their authentically Christian sense.*

∼

The question remains how a highly intelligent Benedictine can fail to recognize the chasm separating the Gospels and the Upanishads, and go so far as, in a way, to identify Buddha and Christ. I surmise that Harry Oldmeadow may have a point when he writes:

> It cannot be too strongly stressed that Abhishiktananda's struggle can only be understood in the context of the times, that is to say, in a period in which Roman legalism, triumphalism, and exclusivism were the order of the day, and in which Latin theology was firmly tied to a religious historicism which identified the historical Jesus and his Church as the only means through which man might find salvation.[3]

3. *A Christian Pilgrim in India* (World Wisdom, 2008), p. 135.

One cannot but concur that it may have been an excess of "Roman legalism, triumphalism, and exclusivism" that contributed to Abhishiktananda's deconversion. What however I find most interesting of all in this quotation is the fact that what Oldmeadow himself decries as "religious historicism" *happens to be a central claim of Christianity*!

What he has to say alerts us thus to the fact that Henri Le Saux may indeed have been touched from the outset by a propensity towards what the pre-Conciliar Church referred to generically as "modernism"—which would go a long way towards explaining his eventual conversion to Vedanta. Whatever namely his emotional attachment to Christianity may have been, a modernist can have no authentic comprehension of *who Christ is* and *what in truth His teaching affirms*. It is not altogether surprising, therefore, that the Psalms, for example, which during an earlier phase of life, Le Saux found inspiring, may eventually strike him as "so very *māyā*," to put it in his own words. Tastes and sentiments do change; it is ultimately our commitment to *truth* that counts.

∽

It happens, moreover, that a diary entry, dated February 1, 1973—just seven months before his death—confirms the aforesaid suspicion: by now, at least, his conception of Christianity is, most assuredly, no longer Christian. Here is what he writes:

> Christ loses nothing of his true greatness when he is delivered from the false grandeurs with which myths

and theological reflections had overlaid him. Jesus is the wondrous epiphany of the mystery of Man, of the *Purusha*, the mystery of every human being, as the Buddha was, and Ramana, and so many others. He is the mystery of the *Purusha* that seeks itself in the cosmos. His epiphany is powerfully marked by the time and place of his appearance in the flesh. He came first of all for the lost ones of the house of Israel as he himself said. Far more than being the "head" of a religion, Jesus is first of all a questioning of every human being. An examination of each one about his relation with God and with his brothers as actually lived. Christian dogma has too often emptied and stolen him from his brothers.

One could, of course, write a substantial essay by way of response; let it suffice to note that once one perceives Christ as a Vedantic sage, such as the Buddha or the Maharshi, one has closed the door to even the most rudimentary comprehension of Christianity. From that point onwards, all that is in fact definitive of Christianity has been jettisoned. Admittedly, Christ can indeed be viewed as a Vedantic sage: the point, however, is that He is infinitely more!

It needs to be understood that this "more" is incomprehensible to the Hindu mind by virtue of the fact that it transcends the Vedic categories: there are no words, even, in the Sanskrit language to express the definitive conceptions of Christianity. It is therefore no wonder that, to the Vedantic or "Vedantized" mind, that "more" is apt to present itself as "false grandeurs with which myths and theological reflections have overlaid him." What *is* surprising is only that a Christian—let alone a priest—should adopt this view. In the case of Henri Le Saux, the question remains whether his conception of Christ and of Christianity was orthodox—or "traditional" if you prefer—prior to his arrival in India, or whether it was heterodox from the start; and this is an issue we happily leave to others to resolve.

What alone concerns us is the fact that *one cannot understand the first thing about Christianity*—and I mean, of course, "as traditionally understood"—*so long as it is viewed from a Vedantic point of vantage*: for in that case one has excluded its very essence, its very heart.

∽

Getting back once more to von Balthasar's prophecy regarding an engagement-to-be between the Christian West and India: the story of Henri Le Saux should suffice to underscore the need and indeed urgency of such a face-to-face encounter. And as a matter of fact, the Benedictine *sādhu* himself testifies to this effect; referring to the implications of *advaita* Vedanta for the religions of the world, he writes:

> The challenge posed to Christianity, as to every form of religion and philosophy, is an ultimate one. They are pursued to their last line of defense and compelled to face an ultimate dilemma—either to remain forever on the level of what is multiple and relative, or to allow their identity to be dissolved in the overwhelming experience of the Absolute.[4]

4. Quoted in Harry Oldmeadow, op. cit., p. 120.

To be sure, one cannot but concur with Abhishiktananda that the challenge posed to Christianity by "eastern religious experience" is indeed ultimate. I decisively disagree however when he claims that the Christian is eventually obliged to "allow his identity to be dissolved in the overwhelming experience of the Absolute": that is to assume from the outset that Christianity is—and indeed *can be*—no more than a "mythologized Vedanta"! But this is precisely the tenet against which we have argued from the outset: it constitutes an outright denial of what the Apostles and the Fathers of the Church—not to speak of Jesus Christ Himself—have taught. It is namely to assume that the Christ-given Eschaton known as Salvation reduces to the *nirvānic* option.

Now, admittedly: once one has "demythologized" the teachings of Christ—negated, that is, every Christic logion which declares otherwise—the sophistical argument is complete. It requires however a very substantial indoctrination in modernist premises before such a train of reasoning can appear to exhibit so much as a semblance of cogency. Once again: *Christianity does not reduce to Vedanta, nor can it be comprehended in Vedantic terms.* To which one might add that it is by no means the destiny of a Christian to be "dissolved"—like Edwin Arnold's dewdrop—"in the overwhelming experience of the Absolute"!

It is time to put an end to this rampant confusion and set the record straight—which is what I propose to do in the next chapter.

3

EXTRA ECCLESIAM NULLA SALUS

Let us reflect, then, on the identity of the Christian Eschaton, named Salvation: what concerns us above all is whether this may conceivably coincide with the Vedic. It is clear from the outset that inasmuch as Christianity was founded by Jesus Christ, this inquiry must be based upon His teachings, and thus primarily upon the Gospels. On that basis, however, the question virtually answers itself; in fact, an incontrovertible proof can be given in five words: "*Salvation is of the Jews*"![1]

These words, spoken by Jesus to the Samaritan woman at the well, refer evidently to a vast chain of events initiated by God's covenant with Abraham, as related in chapter 15 of Genesis: this is where the story of God's Chosen People—and of Christianity—begins. What it relates is something entirely new, something never before seen or heard of on Earth: humanity has been "bisected," as it were, by an Act of God. But why: for what purpose? The fact is that God raised a Chosen People to prepare for the greatest miracle of all time: the *incarnation* of the *Word*. As St. John declares:

---

1. John 4:22. It needs of course to be recalled that the Vedic tradition decisively antedates the Semitic.

> *The Word was made flesh, and dwelt among us, (and we beheld his glory, the glory as of the only begotten of the Father) full of grace and truth.*[2]

Now, this most assuredly is something you absolutely do not find in the Vedas! Of course, I can almost hear it: "What are you saying: what about Sri Krishna, for example?" To be sure, Sri Krishna is what Hindus term an *avatāra*, which is in a way a manifestation of God in human form. But let us not forget that, in a suitably attenuated sense, so is every human being. My point is that by no stretch of the imagination can an *avatāra* be identified with "*the Word made flesh*": the very idea of "the Word" is in fact nowhere to be found in the Vedas! It is simply undeniable that the Trinitarian conception of God was introduced by Jesus Christ.

Getting back to the issue—the identity or non-identity of the Vedic and the Christian Eschaton—let us recognize that John 4:22 (which affirms that "*Salvation is of the Jews*") suffices to resolve the issue: if Salvation were indeed the same as the *nirvāna* proclaimed in the Vedas, it would obviously *not* be "of the Jews."

∽

Salvation not only fails to coincide with the Vedic Eschaton, but differs so categorically as to be actually inconceivable in Vedic terms. It happens namely that the Vedic mindset appears to have no conception of "sin" in the authentic Judeo-Christian sense, nor of the Adamic Fall that has afflicted mankind since history

---

2. John 1:14

began. While the effects of the Fall—the resultant incapacity to "see"—is clearly recognized in the Vedic scriptures, the Fall itself is nowhere acknowledged.[3] The Hindu speaks of *karma*, conceived as the effect of human actions, and distinguishes between "good" and "bad" *karma*; but *sin* and "bad *karma*" are by no means the same, a matter deserving consideration of its own. Suffice it to say that there is a categorical difference between the Vedic and the Christian outlook in that regard, and that the latter is indeed Semitic to the core. Thus, when the Christian speaks, for example, of "the forgiveness of sins," the Hindu has actually not the ghost of an idea what this means. In the end it may be easier for a Christian to catch a glimpse of *advaita* Vedanta than for a Vedantist *not* to misconceive Christianity.

Returning to the pivotal claim that "*Salvation is of the Jews*": this is obviously by no means the only Gospel text permitting us to conclude that the Salvation offered to mankind by Jesus Christ does not reduce to the Vedic Eschaton. In fact, this affirmation pervades the Gospels implicitly much as the drone in Indian music, which is ever present, whether we hear it or not. It was after all to bring Salvation to the world that Jesus Christ was born, that He taught and performed miracles, and ultimately gave up His life upon the Cross.

Let the pundits of ecumenism take note of this fact, and cease ever after to clothe Jesus in the garb of a Vedic sage, or even an *avatāra*—which is to "muddy the

---

3. I have touched upon this issue in *The Vertical Ascent* (Philos-Sophia Initiative Foundation, 2021), the chapter on "The Mystery of Visual Perception."

waters" hopelessly. Even as the Christian intelligentsia has need to open their minds to the mysteries of Vedic spirituality, so does it behoove the Hindus, along with their Occidental confrères, *not* to depict Jesus Christ in the colors of a *rishi*, or confuse Him with an enlightened Sage such as Sri Ramana Maharshi: to do so is to close the door from the start to even the most rudimentary comprehension of Christianity.

~

It should be noted that even the Judeo-Christian cosmology differs radically from the Vedic, which conceives of the cosmos as inherently *cyclic*. In place of an endless sequence of cycles and sub-cycles, Jesus refers emphatically to an actual *termination* of the cosmos at the *Parousia* or Second Coming of Christ. Not only, however, does this teaching break categorically with the Vedic, but it opens the door to a *bona fide* teleology: to the idea, namely, that the cosmos may in truth be more than something that merely exists—or at least appears to do so—but may actually have a purpose: may have an End! In flat contradiction to modern materialism and Vedic cyclicity alike, Christianity proclaims that the cosmos does have in fact an End in both senses of the term. And what is perhaps the most shocking of all to the non-Christian: that End is centered upon *man*.[4]

It appears that God is not all that much concerned with the bigness of the universe, the millions or billions of this and that: what seems ultimately to matter

---

4. On the subject of the *Parousia* I refer to *The Vertical Ascent*, ibid., chapter 12.

is *man*, what our pundits have demoted to the status of a simian who has but recently (and by chance) learned to walk on his hind legs. And the reason for this "centrality" of man—which again is incurably Judeo-Christian—is that he "*was made in the image and likeness of God.*"[5] We are beginning to sense the magnitude of the Christian claim; and perhaps the likeness of a Father is beginning to rise up before our eyes: a Father, that is, *who loves his child*. Slowly no doubt, but irresistibly, the idea of *love* begins to obtrude, as indeed it *must*: for the simple reason that without this pivotal conception it is impossible to understand the first thing about the religion founded by Jesus Christ.

We need moreover to grasp that Christianity is incomparably more than merely a "religion" in the contemporary sense: that it entails in fact a cosmology of its own. I pity the theologians who—with boundless naiveté—accept all the latest oracles put out by the scientific *periti*, and expect, on that basis, to understand the words of Christ! No wonder Christianity is experiencing difficult times—and no wonder too that a contemporary Benedictine speaks of "*false grandeurs with which myths and theological reflection have overlaid*" the Son of God.

It appears that St. Thomas Aquinas was onto something when he remonstrated against the opinion—which apparently was beginning to gain ground even in his day—that it matters not what we believe regarding the cosmos so long as we have a correct view concerning God. Not so, replies the Angelic Doctor: "*because an error regarding the nature of creation always gives rise*

---

5. Gen. 1:26, 27

*to a false idea concerning God.*⁶ One wishes that more of his modern-day followers had paid attention to these words of the Master!

Let me say it, then, once and for all: you cannot begin to comprehend the teaching of Christ unless you grasp the cosmology it entails: *no other cosmology* namely—beginning with the Vedic—*will do*. It is scarcely surprising, therefore, that our modernist savants love to speak of "*myths*," a terminology which serves as a universal panacea: everything we don't understand about Christianity turns forthwith into a "myth": how very convenient!

The Vedic religion has an advantage over Christianity inasmuch as its cosmology is comparatively innocuous: "cyclicity" is in fact a darling of the contemporary scientific mindset, making the Vedic cosmology seem far more up-to-date and superstition-free. The fact that it too does not fit the scientific mold—that the so-called "*law of karma*," for example, is quite as inexplicable to the physicist as, say, the dogma of the "*resurrection*"—does not seem to concern the pundits very much.

It is high time to turn our back to the modern world—its gurus of whatever persuasion—and pay heed to Jesus Christ: we must, at the very least, pay Him the courtesy of not submitting His words to the criteria imposed by the "experts" of our day. Admittedly His teaching is "hard": the problem came up right at the start when He touched upon the incomparable mystery of the Eucharist in the synagogue at Capernaum, speaking the unspeakable; and when He said:

6. *Summa Contra Gentiles*, Bk. II, ch. 3.

"*He that eateth of this bread shall live forever,*" even His disciples "*murmured.*"[7]

No wonder so many of His followers are anxious to "demythologize" His teachings: life would be so much simpler! The disadvantage, however, is that there would then be no such thing as Salvation: there *could not be*.

∽

Let us then get back to the question of teleology, which cannot in fact be "demythologized." In the sharpest conceivable contrast, namely, to the Vedic cosmology, the Christian insists that God made the world for a purpose, for the sake of an End. So far from constituting an endless succession of cycles and sub-cycles, Christ teaches that the universe we behold will terminate abruptly at the *Parousia*—His Second Coming—when both the teleological and the temporal End will be realized. What then, let us ask, is that "teleological End"?

By now it will come as no surprise that this has to do with *eschatology*: with the *salvation*, no less, of *man*. As Jesus said plainly to the Jews at Capernaum:

> *And this is the will of him that sent me, that everyone which seeth the Son, and believeth in him, may have everlasting life: and I will raise him up at the last day.*[8]

To the boundless astonishment of modern man and of the Vedic savants as well: not only does the cosmos

---

7. John 6:53-61
8. John 6:40

have a *purpose*—a *telos*—but that *telos* is *the salvation of man*: of men, women, and children, to be exact. For my part, I can conceive of nothing more drastically at variance with the Vedantic *Weltanschauung*.

Everything Jesus teaches is new; and even when He repeats what the Jewish prophets have said, He gives it a connotation no human mind had previously conceived. No teaching ever before promulgated had endowed man with a destiny even remotely as glorious! Jesus gives us to understand that it is the God-given destiny of man—his very *raison d'être*—to become united with God himself *without forfeiting human nature*. And let us not fail to note, once again, that *herein resides the crucial point of difference between the Vedic and the Christian Eschaton*. To anyone who might nonetheless be tempted to identify the two, I would point to the Christ-given notion of *bodily resurrection* to put the issue to rest: who namely can doubt that the Vedic sages would stand to a man with the pundits on the Areopagus who scoffed at St. Paul!

∼

What is it, then, in the Christian *Weltanschauung*—*in fine finali*—that distinguishes it categorically from the Vedic: could it be the absolute primacy of *man*? I incline to believe that something even more fundamental stands at issue: I surmise it is the primacy of *Love*, the Christian "*Deus caritas est*,"[9] which is nowhere else to be found. The cosmos is there—to the extent that it is—because God "desires" to share his Blessedness, to

---

9. 1 John 4:16

"give himself" if you will, somewhat as parents desire to give themselves to their child. Even as it is definitive of Christian theology to conceive of God as a Father eternally begetting his Son, so also it is a prime characteristic of the Christian God to create men and women in order to bestow upon them his Love.

I am not suggesting by any means that an element of divine *caritas* does not play an essential role in the Vedic religion as well: that would be as foolish as it is misinformed. One need but take a look at the Bhagavad Gitā, for example, to see that it contains an entire chapter on "divine love," in which Arjuna is assured—five times, in fact—that whosoever takes refuge in God is dear to him: "*Exceedingly dear to me are they who regard me as the Supreme Goal*"—so the chapter ends. Clearly, there can in fact be no authentic religion of any kind without an element of divine love entering into play.

On the other hand, the fact that divine *caritas* or *agape* enters the picture in both the Vedic and the Christian religion does not imply that these manifestations are in some sense equivalent. Certainly both religions entail a "return to God," which most assuredly brings an element of love into play; we need however to recall that this "return" is very different in the two cases. Remember the distinction made in chapter 1 between the "dewdrop" and the "wedding feast"!

∼

Christianity is centered—not upon what Vedanta knows as *brahman* or *ātma*—but upon the Incarnate Word, which is never so much as mentioned in all the Vedas. It is centered upon Jesus Christ, who is both

God and man—*true God and true man*, as theology teaches. And not only does Jesus bear love for mankind—as the *Gitā* avers that *brahman* does as well—but He loves to the point of *suffering* for our redemption, which apparently *brahman* does not. To which I would add that this happens *not* to be a myth: in John 12:32, Christ declares:

> *And I, if I be lifted up from the earth, will draw all men unto me.*

To be "*lifted up from the earth*" refers of course to the Crucifixion: Christ was born—came to Earth—in order to be crucified, thus to "*draw all men*" unto Himself. Incidentally: does not this alone distinguish Him categorically from all Hindu *avatāras*? What presently concerns us, however, is the question why the Word that "*was made flesh, and dwelt among us*" had to be crucified: put to death by this most cruel means no less? There are two answers: one refers to the past, the other to the future—and neither is in the least degree comprehensible to the Vedic mind.

The first is that Christ was crucified to atone not only for the Original Sin of Adam, but for all the sins committed subsequently by fallen mankind; and the second is that He was put to death to consummate the greatest miracle of all time; in the marvelous words of the Fathers: "*God became man that man might become God.*" This act of Incarnation began namely with the *Immaculate Conception of the Blessed Virgin Mary* and was consummated in the *Resurrection of Christ her Son*: He that rose from the tomb was indeed the *true God and true Man* who will "*draw all men*" unto Himself.

This recognition places us at the very heart of Christianity, and *ipso facto* at the veritable antipode to the Vedic religion. To put it in the plainest possible terms: instead of man shedding his human nature to return to God, as in the Vedic religion, it now is God *assuming human nature* to unite himself with man.

∽

Needless to say, the spiritual practices pertaining to the two religions clearly reflect this fundamental divergence of the respective Destinations. It is hardly surprising that those who follow the path of Vedanta practice disciplines aimed at disassociating them from their human self: for example, they recite *mantras* such as the *mahāvākya*[10] "*tat tvam asi*"—literally "that thou art"—to this effect. With the erosion of their human identity, moreover, the Christian categories become meaningless: for the *sādhu* in quest of the *advaitic* realization, the teachings of Christ have forfeited their sense. As Swami Abhishiktananda himself observes:

> Even the doctrines of the Trinity and the Incarnation can no longer speak to the soul. The soul is absolutely compelled to lose the Triune God and the God-Man as it had conceived of them, and to allow itself to be swallowed up in the abyss of Being, of the Godhead beyond all conceiving, which attracts it irresistibly.

How well he has put it: herein resides the great divide between the Vedic and the Christian Way. What I find

---

10. The term means literally "great saying."

amazing, on the other hand, is that it never seems to have occurred to this Benedictine, at least in his later years, that the Eschaton of Christianity—the Eschaton instituted by Christ—might *not* reduce to the *nirvānic* option: to a merging into that "abyss of Being" and "Godhead beyond all conceiving" which attracted him so mightily.

However, whether it be the Vedic religion or the Christian, the Eschaton is *perforce* a "seeing" of God: *such a "seeing" constitutes namely a "knowing" which is at once a "being"*—and there is in truth no other *summum bonum* than that. What distinguishes the two religions, thus, is simply the *kind* of "seeing" to which they give access: whether it be unmediated or mediated by the Incarnate Word, a seeing of God directly or in Jesus Christ, his Son. Yet inasmuch as the *being* of the ultimate seer conforms to the *seeing*, that *being* will not be the same in the two modes; and as we have noted repeatedly, only in the Christian Eschaton is it the human person who survives to taste the bliss of immortality.

∽

We have noted that one becomes a Christian through an entry into the Mystical Body of Christ, which is in a sense the *ecclesia*, the Church. And thus interpreted, the ancient dictum *extra ecclesiam nulla salus*—"outside the Church there is no salvation"—emerges as a veritable theorem. But what then are the exact bounds of that *ecclesia*? I wonder whether anyone knows the precise answer to that question but the Lord Himself.

4

BREAKING THE
ĀTMA-MĀYĀ DICHOTOMY

It behooves us to consider the highly prestigious and widely disseminated doctrine often labeled "perennialist," the most influential exponent of which—besides René Guénon—being Frithjof Schuon. As the reader may have noted, much of what we have brought to light thus far speaks against that doctrine; it is however time to take a closer look. Let me begin with a quotation from the master himself:

> According to certain Fathers of the Church, "God became man so that man might become God"; an audacious and elliptical formula which we might paraphrase in a Vedantic fashion by saying that the Real became illusory so that the illusory might become real: *ātma* became *māyā* so that *māyā* might realize *ātma*. This is the very definition of Revelation and the Revealer; of *dharma* and of the *avatāra*.[1]

It strikes me that these observations hinge on an assumption which proves ultimately to be untenable:

---

1. "The Perennial Philosophy," *The Unanimous Tradition* (Sri Lanka Institute of Traditional Studies, 1991), p. 21.

Schuon seems namely to presuppose that one can comprehend the truth of Christianity in Vedantic terms. But that turns out to be a very big assumption! Granting that one can argue in behalf of the so-called "transcendent unity of religions," one can also question the validity of these arguments and espouse the opposing view, which is what we propose to do. To begin with, we reject the *ātma-māyā* dichotomy on the grounds that the teachings of Christ transcend these Vedantic categories, a case in point being the Christian Eschaton itself, which does not in truth reduce to either term.

Let us begin with Schuon's paraphrase of the Incarnation as "the Real" becoming "illusory": there is no way a Christian can accept this contention, which in fact he is bound to perceive as the very inversion of the truth. When "*the Word was made flesh, and dwelt among us,*" it most certainly did not cease to be *the Word*! The point is that Christ became—not "*the darkness*"—but rather "*the light that shines in the darkness.*" And whereas "*the darkness comprehended it not,*" those who were "of the light" did, and in fact "*beheld His glory, the glory as of the only begotten of the Father, full of grace and truth.*"[2]

Admittedly Vedanta does not recognize the possibility of the Incarnation; but what exactly does this prove, other than the fact that we are confronted by two different religions! What this discrepancy actually brings to light, it seems to me, is not a so-called "*transcendent unity*" of the two religions, but indeed their

2. John 1:14

radical disparity. And for my part, I see nothing in the least surprising or incongruous in that: when, after all, did God ever proclaim Vedanta and Christianity to be one and the same! At bottom Schuon's approach strikes me as Procrustean: what does not fit the Vedantic mold must be "amputated."

As we have already had occasion to note, the Incarnation proves in fact to be something categorically different from the Vedantic *avatāra*: so far, namely, from constituting "*true God and true man*" in the Christian sense, the human side of the *avatāra* is indeed relegated by the savants of Vedanta to the realm of *māyā*. To the extent, therefore, that one absolutizes this teaching, one is obliged to deny the Christian claim: and to be sure, this is what major segments of our Western intelligentsia have been doing for quite a long time.

What I wish to point out, first of all, is that in taking this stance, they are contradicting not only the teachings of Christianity, but of the integral Vedic tradition itself: for as we have pointed out in chapter 2, the latter refuses to absolutize the Vedanta, but conceives of it rather as a so-called *darśana*, what could almost be termed a "point of view." We must never forget that the ultimate truth enshrined in the Vedic tradition cannot in fact be fully grasped this side of the *chittavrittinirodha*. In the final count, it appears that Schuon may have misread not only the Christian religion, but the Vedic as well, which he seems to view through Occidental eyes.

We have already commented on the antipodal nature of the Vedic and the Christian Eschaton. Yet it needs also to be noted that the last word in the Vedic tradition, so far from being in any sense "sectarian," proves rather to be its ubiquitous "*neti, neti*": that underlying drone of "not so, not so" which negates not only the "is," but equally the "is not" of all things our earthly minds can conceive. And whereas this implicit double negation constitutes, in a way, the doctrinal adjunct of the yogic path, it strikes the Occidental mind as something quite incongruous. All of us have, presumably, encountered indigenous aficionados of *advaita* Vedanta passionately defending this or that doctrinal claim, based supposedly on the "truth of Vedanta": suffice it to note, however, that to the authentic Oriental mind such a dogmatic affirmation may in fact raise what the Zen master refers to as "little lumps of doubt."

∼

Getting back to Frithjof Schuon's "transcendent unity" thesis: what we find problematic in his reading of the Incarnation as "*ātma* become *māyā*" is the implicit assumption that, what is not *ātma* is *ipso facto māyā*, a supposition I deem to be untenable. Christianity, in particular, does break that *ātma-māyā* dichotomy: it does so, namely, by virtue of its Trinitarian theology. It is the Logos, let us recall, which enters the cosmos as "*the light that shineth in darkness*," or as "the Real within *māyā*" one might also say. What Schuon has apparently left out of the picture is the Word that "*was made flesh, and dwelt among us*": it seems that, when great men err, it is not over trifles.

One needs to recall that Christian doctrine rests squarely upon the Trinitarian theology first revealed to mankind by Jesus Christ, a fact which has two major corollaries: first, that this doctrine is nowhere to be found in the Vedic tradition; and secondly, that it transcends the limitations of the "merely human," which is to say that it survives the *chittavrittinirodha*. As Christ Himself declares: "*Heaven and earth shall pass away, but my words shall not pass away.*"[3] And let us not fail to note that no such claim is to be found in the Vedic tradition, a fact which elevates the teachings of Christ above the status of a Vedic *darśana*, and *de jure* exempts that teaching from the "*neti, neti*" censure.

∽

One sees in retrospect that the Schuonian thesis attacks Christianity at its very core by *de facto* denying the possibility of the Incarnation: its implicit claim that Christ transcends the *ātma-māyā* dichotomy in a way Vedanta cannot so much as conceive. What in point of fact, however, renders Christianity invulnerable to that charge proves to be its Trinitarian theology: no lesser theology, it appears, could withstand the Vedantic onslaught. What renders the Vedantic ontology incapable in that regard is precisely its lack of a *tertium quid* to mediate between the *ātma-māyā* antipodes. It can also be argued, on the other hand, that to absolutize that Vedantic duality is already to misread the Vedic claim, which is only authentic so long as it is accompanied by that unceasing "*neti, neti*" refrain.

Let us realize that Vedanta and Christianity constitute indeed two very different religions, to the point of being in a way antipodal, as in fact we have had ample

---

3. Matt. 24:35, Mark 13:31; as also, "*The words that I speak unto you, they are spirit, and they are life*" (John 6:63).

occasion to note.[4] One is of course at liberty to suppose that Christianity is based upon a lie; to do so, however, is hardly to prove the so-called "transcendent unity of religions."

∼

The most direct—and also, I am persuaded, the most enlightening—way to comprehend how Trinitarian theology enters the picture to the detriment of Schuon's claims is to avail oneself of Meister Eckhart's stupendous discovery, his utterly amazing exegesis of Psalm 61:12: "*God has spoken once and for all, and I have heard two things.*"[5] And as a matter of fact, this exegesis puts us directly on Vedantic ground by its recognition of the sense-perceived cosmos as *māyā* in precisely the Vedantic sense: as something, namely, that vanishes upon the accomplishment of the *chittavrittinirodha*. There is perfect agreement, in that regard, between Vedanta and Christianity conceived on its most profoundly esoteric plane. Where the two religions differ, on the other hand, is in their reading of what remains following the *nirodha*: what the Vedanta declares to be *ātma*, Christianity takes to be "*Father-and-Son*," something that, strictly speaking, is "neither 1 nor 2." And therein, I take it, resides the key difference that elevates Christianity above the Vedic religion. One might say that "beyond the realm of *chittavritti*," what logicians term "the law of the excluded middle" does not apply: it is broken, in effect, by what Christianity knows as the Trinity.

4. We are referring especially to sections I and II of chapter 1.
5. We refer again to chapter 1, part III

The marvel of Meister Eckhart's exegesis is that it displays this discrepancy between the Vedic and the Christian ontology with perfect precision. One sees, in the first place, that what "*God has spoken once and for all*" is none other than his "*only-begotten Son*": namely "*the Word that was in the beginning*," which proves to be the tertiary element missing from the Vedantic *ātma-māyā* dichotomy. On the other hand, "*the second thing I have heard*"—which does not in truth exist because "*God has spoken once and for all*"—is none other than the illusory world of *māyā*, which it is the function of *yoga* to dispel. What thus, according to Christianity, survives the *nirodha* is not only the Father—corresponding in a way to what the Vedanta takes to be *ātma*—but includes in addition the Logos: "*the Word that was in the beginning*," which is Christ Himself. It turns out that Eckhart's flash of genius gives us the full picture at a single stroke.

The upshot is this: where the Vedanta sees only *ātma*, Christianity recognizes *God the Father and God the Son, united by the Holy Spirit*. And it is this definitive recognition that validates the Christian concept of the Incarnation—which proves indeed not to be conceivable in Vedic terms—and in so doing, refutes Schuon's "*ātma* became *māyā*" interpretation thereof.

∽

It is on this Trinitarian basis—and on this basis alone!—that the Christian doctrine of the *Incarnation* can be adequately comprehended; and most assuredly, it does *not* reduce to Vedic terms. On the contrary: it follows that inasmuch as "*I and my Father are one*," the *Incarnation* encompasses ultimately *all* of Reality, both "outside" and "within" *māyā*. And so, too, we are now in a position to recognize, once again, that the way of Christianity constitutes the one and only means to exit from the realm of *māyā* without submitting to the Vedantic self-immolation: it appears that Christ, in the infinitude of His Love, has in a way accomplished this for us. So far from "*ātma* becoming *māyā*," one sees that the *Incarnation* is in truth the "terminator of *māyā*," who would save us from its deadly sway.

The supreme miracle upon which Christianity rests—the Incarnation, namely, which is indeed *true God and true man* in the most literally accurate sense—remains perforce incomprehensible to the Vedantist. That Christ, as the *Logos*, is *true God* we know on the basis of Trinitarian theology; and that He is, at the same time, *true man* we know from the fact that "*God has spoken once and for all.*" In the final count, all things exist *in Christo* to the extent that they exist at all. It is this metaphysical fact, moreover, that validates the Christian "Way of Salvation": Christ is indeed the Savior because the reality of who we are resides in Him. One might say that not only is there no salvation "*extra ecclesiam*," but that "outside of Christ" man does in truth "reduce to *māyā*."

Such is the Christian teaching, the Christian view; and admittedly it does not conform to the Vedantic. But, by the same token, neither does the Vedantic view conform to the Christian. If, then, an authentic "unity of religions" were to exist, it must indeed be radically "transcendent"! Schuon's mistake, it appears to me, was to absolutize the Vedanta: to take it as the absolute truth. To do so is not only at variance with the claims of

Christianity, but with the Vedic teaching itself, which refuses to absolutize any *darśana*.

∽

To round out the picture of Christianity, we need to remind ourselves that the teachings of Christ do not stand alone, but constitute the summit and fulfillment of the Judeo-Christian tradition, to which also it holds the key. "A collection of myths," our *periti* will say: there has been a concerted movement namely, in force since the Enlightenment, to "demythologize" religious beliefs in the name of "science." Suffice it to note that not only have we argued for years that these claims are spurious, but have insisted at the same time that authentic myth is in fact "the nearest approach to absolute truth that can be expressed in words," to quote Ananda Coomaraswamy.

It needs also however to be understood that authentic myth does not, strictly speaking, reduce to words—no more than a melody, for example, reduces to its notes. And even as there are individuals who hear the notes but remain deaf to the melody, so too it is in the case of myth. To ascend beyond the words or notes—to receive the irreducible wholeness[6] these "carry"—something is evidently demanded of the percipient himself. And the point is essential; as Christ declares: *"He that hath, to him shall be given."* Admittedly, this teaching may strike

---

6. Regarding this concept I refer to my article "Irreducible Wholeness and Dembski's Theorem," *Philos-Sophia Initiative*, 11 March 2021. See philos-sophia.org/irreducible-wholeness-dembski-theorem.

us as rather "undemocratic" or "discriminatory"[7]—and yet the fact remains that something too is demanded of the recipient: in the final count, there is no such thing as a "free lunch."

Getting back to the Judeo-Christian tradition: it is to be understood that this adjunct of Christianity is not "merely" an historical precursor—nor, indeed, "merely" anything at all—but proves to be integral to the truth of Christianity. What I wish to point out, in particular, is that the "myth of Adam" stands at the very center of the Christian teaching as indeed "the nearest approach to absolute truth that can be stated in words." I shall argue, in fact, that in a way this "myth" itself *resolves the impasse of the Vedantic ātma-māyā dichotomy*. Instead of that dichotomy "invalidating Christianity"—as some perennialists seem to think—the table has turned: it is now Christianity that, in a sense, "invalidates" Vedanta by virtue of the fact that Adam *transcends the ātma-māyā dichotomy*. And let us note that, whereas this may come as a shock to our Occidental Vedantists, it accords actually with the *authentic* Vedic tradition, which as we have noted repeatedly, regards the Vedanta as simply one *darśana* out of six, to be exact.

It may not be without interest to recall, moreover, that the six *darśanas* are traditionally associated with the six "directions of space," and that the Vedanta corresponds to the vertically upward, which is indeed—quite literally—"the highest." Yet, even so, this *darśana*

---

7. One might mention that the second half of this Christic logion (Matt. 13:12) sounds even more offensive to contemporary ears: to take away from "*whosoever hath not*" even "*the little that he has*"—that is about as bad as things can get!

cannot stand alone. The pundits acknowledge, for example, that the so-called *tanmātras* or "subtle elements," which form the basis of sense-perception, are in fact invisible to the Vedanta. To detect these *tanmātras* one requires another *darśana*: the Sānkhya namely. My point is that no single *darśana* is all-sufficing.

It appears that our *periti* have it backwards: in their reduction of Christianity to Vedanta, they presume to comprehend the "greater" in terms of the "lesser." On the side of the Judeo-Christian "more" one can mention: first, the Trinitarian theology as revealed by Jesus Christ; and, in second place, the story of Adam, which we take to be a *bona fide* myth in the sense of Ananda Coomaraswamy. Having already noted that the former breaks the Vedantic *ātma-māyā* dichotomy, we would like now to point out that the myth of Adam does so as well. It does so by virtue of the Fall: as the instrumental cause of *māyā*, Adam has ontological precedence. Once again we discover the worldview of the Judeo-Christian tradition to be wider than the Vedic: it appears, namely, that the Vedic tradition knows nothing about the Fall.[8] No wonder it "absolutizes" *māyā*!

∼

One sees, from a Christian point of vantage, that "*māyā*" is no longer a primary category, and what in a sense takes its place proves indeed to be *man*: the *anthropos* who constitutes a "microcosm" in himself. And needless to say, this changes everything—beginning with

---

8. I have touched upon that issue in *The Vertical Ascent* (Philos-Sophia Initiative Foundation, 2021), chapter 10.

the fact that, instead of *man* being in some way derived from *māyā*, the matter actually stands the other way round.

It is to be noted that, by virtue of this shift—from *māyā* to the *anthropos*—the cosmos admits a *telos*: it is there for a purpose, an End. And this accounts, on the plane of cosmology, for the shift from the unending cyclicity of the Vedic cosmos to the non-cyclicity entailed by the *Parousia*: the fact that, at the Second Coming of Christ, the cosmos will come to an End, as He declares.

Here, in these radically divergent cosmic scenarios, we see a reflection of the gargantuan disparity between the two religions! And clearly, everyone will ultimately have to make his choice: it is namely inconceivable that they can be "equally true." Again, the "antipodal" nature of the two religions stares us in the face! On the one hand there is the Vedic revelation, proclaiming—by its unending cyclic repetitions—the nonexistence of an Eschaton this side of the *ātma-māyā* divide; and on the other we have the Christian, enjoining us to prepare for the End that shall befall us at the *Parousia*—the "*day and hour*" of which no man knows.

According to the teachings of Christ, the cosmos has a temporal ending because it has a *teleological* End: a *purpose*, that is; and permit me to say that the absence of a cosmic teleology in the Vedic religion has always struck me as a deficiency. It may be the Occidental DNA, but I am troubled by an unresolvable doubt: if the cosmos has no *raison d'être*, why then is it there?

In any case, this problem—if such it be—disappears in Christianity. God "creates the world"—not haphazardly, let alone out of necessity—but for a reason: the most wonderful reason, in fact! He does so to "share his blessedness," to "give himself" to another—even as a father gives himself to his child. And this explains "the centrality of Adam," which derives from the fact that *man—made in the image and likeness of God*—is in a sense, potentially at least, a *child* of Almighty God. Is it any wonder that God loves man: even a "sinner"! And is it any wonder, too, that *man*—in the degree to which he is purified—"*loves God*" in turn?

One sees that, in Christianity, *māyā* is not, after all, a primary principle: what in a way replaces it in the Christian epiphany is the divine *caritas*, the Love that moves God to give himself to another—even at the cost of a supreme and humanly inconceivable Sacrifice. And needless to say, this divine drama of "self-giving," indigenous to Christianity, stands at the very antipode of the *māyā*-world: there is nothing in fact more truly God-like than this supreme *agape*, manifested in the Birth and Death of Christ.

Admittedly, *māyā* does yet enter the picture: but in the greatly reduced capacity of an *effect* which proves to be ultimately what Christianity has labeled a *felix culpa*: a "happy fault" no less. For the "myth of Adam" identifies *māyā*, first, as constituting indeed "*the wages of sin*," which however inaugurates the *salvation* of mankind.

The "myth of Adam" distinguishes thus between three kinds or "stages" of humanity: a "paradisal" or Edenic, exemplified by Adam prior to the Fall; a "fallen," subject to the illusions of *māyā* resulting therefrom; and finally a "*deified*" state which realizes the *telos* or true End of the entire drama—a *summum bonum* which is evidently missing in the Vedantic scenario.

∼

We have moved a long distance from the worldview of those who would reduce Christianity to the Vedantic categories. We have argued not only that such a reduction is misconceived, but that it constitutes an inversion of the truth: a futile effort to comprehend the "more" in terms of the "less." Yet even so, that movement may have a role to play in preparing the ground for the next—and perhaps indeed, the ultimate—form of Christianity, which appears to be in process of formation. Everyone seems to sense that profound changes are in the offing; and for my part, I cannot doubt that the decisive event is bound to be what might properly be termed a "rediscovery of esoterism" within the very heart of Christianity.

And on this point it appears that Frithjof Schuon was absolutely right: most assuredly we concur that no religion can survive, in the long run, without access to a *bona fide* esoterism, acknowledged by at least a core segment of its leadership. To put it in scriptural terms: in addition to Peter, the "*rock*," Christianity has need also for John, the Beloved Disciple, to whom alone it was given to lay his head on the breast of the Savior.[9]

And this brings us back, full circle, to the prophesy of Hans Urs von Balthasar: the only way, namely, Christianity can defend its position in an encounter

---

9. See John 13:23 and 21:20-3. Scant though they be, these references appear to be pivotal.

with the Vedic tradition is on esoteric ground. Even the wisdom of the Angelic Doctor will not quite suffice: it too stands "this side" of the great divide—as the Doctor himself confided to Reginald. At the end of the day we have need of the Meister: the one from whom God is said to have "hidden nothing." And as we have come to see, the Eckhartian exegesis does in fact break the confines of the exoteric: by its Christian comprehension of the *chittavrittinirodha* it has rendered possible an encounter between the Vedic and the Christian wisdom on a common plane, which in principle alters the spiritual landscape decisively. For whereas that Eckhartian exegesis exhibits the primacy of the Judeo-Christian tradition, it precludes all manner of narrow and sectarian opinions which would betray the authentic catholicity of the Christian religion.

It appears, moreover, that von Balthasar may well be right in suggesting that the impact upon the Church of that encounter with India may exceed even that of Greek philosophy following its erstwhile encounter with Greece. One might go so far as to maintain that Meister Eckhart, having in a sense "exited *māyā*" through his exegesis, has opened the way to a Christian understanding of Vedanta, which is the polar opposite of the perennialist reduction. It may not be too much to suggest that, by the depth of his comprehension, the Meister has in fact opened the door to a Trinitarian understanding of *ātma* itself.

Finally I would point out that Christianity, on its most profoundly esoteric plane, is likewise cognizant of *māyā*, which like the Vedanta, Meister Eckhart identifies with the *chittavritti*. Yet the complement of that *māyā*—which might be termed the Trinitarian realm—proves to be incomparably richer than the Vedantic *ātma* inasmuch as it stands to the latter somewhat as the Trinity stands to the Father alone. What is missing in the Vedantic purview is, first of all, the Son—the Second Person of the Trinity—who, as we have seen, breaks the *ātma-māyā* dichotomy, together with the Holy Spirit who completes the Trinity.

Finally, it is by virtue of this Trinitarian mystery that the fateful encounter between "*He that is*" and "*she that is not*" takes place, to quote again the words of Christ to St. Catherine of Siena. And it appears the Patristic theologians did have it right: the End of that encounter is indeed "*the deification of man.*"

5

LOGOCENTRIC METAPHYSICS

If all reality derives from the Logos—if, as "*the light that shineth in darkness*," the Logos pervades all things—it follows that the true metaphysics *must* be Logocentric: must in fact reduce to the metaphysics exposed in the Prologue of St. John, beginning with the words: "*In principio erat Verbum.*"[1]

This metaphysics has been recognized in varying degrees, beginning with the great Patristic savants; for instance, by St. Augustine when he declares:[2]

> *I beheld these others beneath thee, and saw that they neither altogether are, nor altogether are not. An existence they have, because they are from thee; and yet no existence, because they are not what thou art.*

In fact, to say that things exist insofar as "*they are from thee*," yet "*have no existence because they are not what thou art*"—this actually leaves "Logocentric metaphysics" as the one and only viable option. Nor should this come as a surprise: in the very first chapter of Genesis, after all,

---

1. We shall henceforth use the term "Logocentric" in precisely this sense.
2. *Confessions*, VII, 11.

we learn that God created all things by way of *speech*: God *spoke*, and *they were made*. What is "spoken," namely, is again a "*word*."

Our minds, however, tend to be too "scattered" to grasp this crucial point: we are apt to be blinded by the divine simplicity. We have paid insufficient heed to the admonition of Christ to become "*as a little child*," nor have we comprehended the point of His words: "*When thine eye is single, thy whole body also is filled with light*."[3] What the "*single eye*" receives is the "*light that shineth in the darkness*," which "*the darkness comprehended not*." Moreover, Meister Eckhart's exegesis makes it clear that what in fact renders the *eye* "*single*" can ultimately be none other than the *chittavrittinirodha*: it is, after all, this *nirodha* that in the end enables "*the pure in heart*" to "*see God*."[4]

It follows again that the ultimate metaphysics must be "Logocentric" for the very simple reason that the Logos is indeed the *truth*. Christ alone "survives" the *chittavrittinirodha*, along with all who are sacramentally united with Him by way of His "Mystical Body." And this doctrine has been with us for a very long time: from the "*ego sum qui sum*" of Exodus 3:14, if you will, to the explicit disclosure by Christ that He is indeed "*the way, the truth, and the life*."[5] It is high time to grasp the point: to recognize that *the reality of all that exists resides in the Logos itself*.

---

3. Luke 11:34
4. See chapter 1, part III.
5. John 14:6

For a Christian, the fact that the ultimate ontology must be Logocentric stands thus *de jure* above dispute. And as we have had occasion to note, this metaphysical fact—which pertains incurably to the esoteric realm—was indeed acknowledged by the great masters right through the High Middle Ages. We still find it luminously expressed in Hugh of St. Victor (1096-1141) for example: "Each created being," he writes with admirable clarity, "is a symbol instituted, not by the arbitrariness of men, but by the divine will, to render visible the invisible wisdom of God."[6] The decisive point, however, is not that created things, by virtue of their existence, render visible the wisdom of God, but rather that *they exist precisely by virtue of that symbolic act*. In a word: like his predecessor St. Augustine, Hugh of St. Victor was indeed an advocate of Logocentric metaphysics.

Yet the time was fast approaching when Christian esoterism would virtually disappear, at least in the West. St. Thomas Aquinas himself seems to bear witness to this trend by the fact that he apparently consigned his own written opus to the category of "mere straw"—as which it might indeed appear from the yonder side of the *chittavrittinirodha*. My point is that the Angelic Doctor stands at the end of an era, a case indeed of "*après moi le déluge*": what confronts us in the aftermath is in truth a drastic decline. To be precise, it is the rise

---

6. Needless to say, "the invisible wisdom of God" is indeed the Logos. What Hugh of St. Victor affirms is that "created beings" are *symbols* of the Logos—which is indeed precisely what Logocentric ontology contends.

of humanism and of science—in a word, the Enlightenment. By stages and degrees, one arrives inevitably at the position so well-articulated by Albert Einstein in the dictum: "Science deals with what *is*, religion with what *ought to be*."

The scandal is that there are Christians—even in high places—who believe this to be true: how, namely, is it possible to follow Him who *is* "*the truth*" and yet believe that religion deals simply with "what ought to be"! And as to the first part of the Einsteinian dictum, let me note that science is in fact *rigorously incapable* of dealing with "what *is*." As I have argued for years, physical science deals actually—not indeed with what *is*—but precisely with what proves, in some sense, to be *measurable*—which is something else entirely. The truth of the matter is that physical science deals perforce with what, under certain conditions, *appears to be*, whereas it is the prerogative of authentic religion to bring us to a knowledge of that which "*is*." The "*ought to be*" has of course its place; yet, unquestionably, "*what is*" takes precedence.

There has been, I believe, in modern times an overemphasis upon the moral teaching of Christ, to the neglect of the metaphysical. It is almost as if the proponents of Christianity were hesitant to confess the ontological content of their beliefs for fear of ridicule from the scientific sector: when it comes to the question "what *is*"—as distinguished from "what *ought to be*"—our churchmen seem typically to live in fear of the scientist. I have tried for years to get the message across that there is *de jure* no need for these trepidations: that no one in truth knows more about "what *is*" than He who created all things—yet it seems the diffidence born of uncertainty remains.

∼

I wish now to point out that an eminent exponent of Logocentric metaphysics has in fact made his appearance in the twentieth century; I am referring to the French metaphysician Jean Borella. Perhaps not too well known as yet in the English-speaking world, he ranks unquestionably among the most profound and seminal savants of our time.[7] A born philosopher, Borella may be characterized, by his own account, as "instinctively Platonist." It appears that at the age of fourteen he was already occupied with the *Meditations* of Descartes, and by the time he encountered the writings of René Guénon during his college years, he discerned that the latter was, in essence, expounding the Platonist metaphysics "such as I discovered in myself."[8] Yet, even so, the encounter with Guénon has had a decisive impact upon the young philosopher. One may presume that it helped immensely to clarify the metaphysical intuitions native to his intellect, and enabled him, at the same time, to acquire a profound grasp of the Vedantic, Taoist, and Islamic doctrines, of an authenticity and penetration rarely to be met in the

---

7. Some of what we say in the sequel repeats what I wrote in the Foreword to Borella's *The Secret of the Christian Way* (SUNY Press, 2001). As an introduction to the metaphysics of Jean Borella we recommend Bruno Bérard, *A Metaphysics of the Christian Mystery* (Angelico Press, 2018).

8. From an interview published in *L'Age d'Or*.

West. It is also however vital to note that Borella has never acquiesced to Guénon when it comes to Christianity, and has remained all along staunchly orthodox in his religious and theological orientation.[9] Even so, the contact with Guénon, and thus with the Oriental traditions, has doubtless provided a powerful stimulus—a veritable imperative—to deepen and universalize his understanding of the Christian religion. And in point of fact, one encounters in the writings of Jean Borella a comprehension of Christian doctrine freed from even the slightest trace of what might be termed Occidental provincialism.

A Catholic by birth and innermost conviction, Borella evinces an ability to penetrate into the innermost depths of Christianity, right down to its Patristic and Apostolic roots. And it is here, on this primary level, that this instinctively Platonist philosopher came to discover what he terms a "metaphysics of symbolic reference," which not only earned him the coveted *doctorat d'Etat*, but proves to be indeed a Logocentric metaphysics.

~

9. Borella has dealt at length with this issue in *Esotérisme guénonien et mystère chrétien* (an English translation of which has been published by Sophia Perennis in 2004), which gives a masterful refutation of Guénon's views regarding Christianity. In the venerable tradition of the *adversus haereses* treatises of old, Borella utilizes the occasion of a subtle heresy for the unfolding of Christian truth. I should add, however, that this in no wise diminishes Borella's high regard for Guénon as a metaphysician and interpreter of occult and Oriental wisdom.

In a small separate work entitled *Symbolisme et réalité*, published in 1997, Borella recounts the unfolding of his philosophic thought. He begins by recalling the proclamation, delivered in 1950, by Pope Pius XII, which affirms dogmatically that "*Mary, after having completed the course of her earthly life, was raised up, body and soul, to heavenly glory.*" A student of philosophy at the time, he was struck by the fact that this dogma was poorly received even by his fellow Catholics, the dispute centering upon the term "*body.*" Had not Rudolf Bultmann already declared that one cannot "turn on a radio" and still believe that Jesus "ascended" as the Church maintains? "In actuality," Borella explains, "by our scientific certainties and their accompanying mental attitudes, all of us find it extremely difficult to believe in the truth of those sacred facts related to us by the Old and New Testaments. My entire philosophic thrust has sprung from the conviction which has imposed upon me the duty to speculatively accept this formidable challenge." As Borella goes on to relate, the widespread skepticism regarding the dogma of the Assumption and other Christian mysteries

> elicited from me what seemed to be a self-evident response: beyond the divisions and oppositions of analytic reason stands the truth of the real, one with itself, inseparably both historical and symbolic, visible and invisible, corporeal and semantic. This self-evident response rested upon a kind of direct and instantaneous intuition in which was revealed, obscurely but without any possible doubt,

the *ontologically spiritual nature of the matter of bodies*[10] without for all that casting any doubt on the reality of their corporeity.

We may take it that what Borella refers to in this remarkable confession constitutes indeed the decisive intuition—bordering upon the mystical—which has given rise, first to his doctoral dissertation, followed by the full sweep of his literary production. It may not be too far afield to suggest that the entire doctrine Borella is unfolding in book after book is synthetically contained in that "direct and sudden intuition" which first struck the philosopher, at the age of 20, in the wake of the papal proclamation. Moreover, one need but reflect upon the words "*inseparably both historical and symbolic, visible and invisible, corporeal and semantic*" to recognize with certainty that what stands at issue can indeed be nothing short of a literally Logocentric metaphysics.

By the same token, however, it requires a corresponding intuition on the part of the reader to grasp the point of what Borella has to say. His is namely a "top-down" theory in which the whole needs to be grasped "above"—and thus in a way "prior" to—the parts. But such a comprehension demands itself "a direct and sudden" intuition, which is to say that it can be effected only by means of the veritable intellect: that "*single eye*" alluded to by Christ.[11] Like it or not, the fact remains that "*whosoever hath, to him shall be given.*"[12] To comprehend Borella's Logocentric metaphysics one must

---

10. Italics mine.
11. Luke 11:34
12. Matt. 13:12

share to some degree his "direct and instantaneous intuition"—which proves to be the key.

∼

Unprecedented though it be in contemporary times, Borella's metaphysics pertains *de jure* to the great traditions of Christianity. It appears in fact to enshrine the same spiritual vision that inspired Hugh of St. Victor, for example, to declare "*each created being*" to be "*a symbol instituted, not by the arbitrariness of men, but by the divine will, to render visible the wisdom of God.*" To say, namely, of *created beings* at large that they "*render visible the wisdom of God*" is in truth to perceive cosmic reality as "*inseparably both historical and symbolic, visible and invisible, corporeal and semantic.*" What Borella refers to as "*the ontologically spiritual nature of the matter of bodies*" is not anybody's speculation, but a spiritual fact, perceptible to those who have penetrated the teachings of Christ in sufficient depth.

To be sure, the point at issue is exceedingly subtle: it affirms that corporeal entities, say, are neither "light" nor "darkness"—neither *being* nor *nonbeing*—but partake somehow of "light" and "darkness" at once. We need thus to distinguish between the *light* as such[13]— which corporeal entities, most assuredly, are not—and "*light shining in darkness*": for *that* is what the beings or entities of this world prove ultimately to be. It is in truth exactly as St. Augustine states: "*An existence they have, because they are from thee; and yet no existence, because they are not what thou art.*" One might say: "An

---

13. The allusion here is to John 1:5.

existence they have by virtue of the *light*; and yet no existence, on account of the *darkness*."

What is it, then, that corresponds to *māyā*: is it the "*light shining in darkness*," or is it the "*darkness*" itself? For my part, I would opt for the second alternative—but this is a question we need not pursue. Suffice it to say that *māyā* derives from the darkness as the source of "nonbeing."

Getting back to Borella's Logocentric metaphysics: one can, in retrospect at least, recognize the central idea of that metaphysics as indigenous to Christian esoterism *per se*. It is, after all, expressive of the Judeo-Christian ontology as enunciated, for instance, in Exodus 3:14, which Christ reaffirms in the words: "*I am the truth*." But whereas, with the Enlightenment, that metaphysical fact has evidently fallen into oblivion, it was yet distinctly recognized right through the High Middle Ages, along with the concomitant fact that the concept of *truth* applies not only to propositions, but to "things" as well. It is one of the forgotten glories of Scholastic philosophy that this tradition ranks "truth" as one of the five so-called *transcendentals* applicable to all *being*. According to the traditional formula, *omnes ens est verum*; or as St. Thomas has it: *omnis res est vera*.[14] A profound kinship, here, with Jean Borella's "symbolic realism" is indisputable. And as one can readily surmise, the implications of this realism are simply boundless: there is hardly a metaphysical question which is not illuminated, and indeed profoundly transformed by this absolutely foundational recognition.

14. *De Veritate*, Q. 1, Art. 10.

I wish finally to point out that Borella's doctrine transgresses "philosophy" as currently conceived, insofar as it does not—cannot in fact—reduce to a purely rational discipline: it appeals, namely, perforce to sacred symbols as immediate "presentifications" of the Real. It thus regards the "offending" dogmas of traditional theology in a manner exactly opposite to the reductionism of the "demythologizers": by the very fact that these dogmatic tenets are void of "scientific" or "empirical" meaning, it recognizes these affirmations as authentic symbols, *irreplaceable as indicators of metaphysical reality.* What strikes the "emancipated" exegete as something categorically nonfactual—something that supposedly is no longer credible after one has "turned on a radio"—may prove thus to constitute, in reality, a bridge that leads the spiritual seeker beyond the confines of the phenomenal realm: beyond what Vedantists refer to as *māyā*. But needless to say: sacred symbols fulfill this lofty function only for those who *believe*, a case indeed of *"credo ut intelligam."*[15] It may not be too much to claim that all authentic Christian belief hinges *in fine finali* upon this principle, in accordance with the Christic logion: "*Whosoever hath, to him shall be given.*"

∼

We are finally in a position to appreciate the vital role of Scripture as a key element of Christianity. It is imperative to realize that Scripture is not in truth situated "within *māyā*," but that in a sense it survives

---

15. "I believe so that I may understand."

the *chittavrittinirodha*; as Christ Himself explains: "*Heaven and earth shall pass away, but my words shall not pass away.*"[16] Everything hinges upon this crucial fact, which tells us that the words of Christ *transcend māyā*. The words of Scripture—and thus the fundamental dogmatic teachings of Christianity—surpass *māyā* by virtue of the fact that they are the "*words*" of Christ that "*shall not pass away.*" They pertain thus—not to the illusory "world" of the *chittavritti*, which ultimately disappears—but to what "*God has spoken once and for all.*" They are indeed "*in the world, but not of it*" in the most literal sense. A crude metaphor would be that of a "rope" cast into a dark labyrinth—or if you will, into Plato's "cave"—by means of which its "prisoners" can find their way out. We need not, however, resort to metaphors: we have after all the words of Christ that "*shall not pass away,*" which lead us directly to the "*truth*" that shall "*make you free.*"[17] And that "*truth*" is Christ Himself.[18]

---

16. Matt. 24:35, Mark 13:31
17. John 8:32
18. John 14:6

POSTSCRIPT

Having shared my recollections of certain Vedantic adepts, let me conclude with my impressions of a twentieth century Christian saint, whom I was also privileged to encounter in that early phase of my life. I am referring to a Capuchin monk known as Padre Pio, who has since been canonized as St. Pius of Pietrelcina. Having heard of him from a friend, I made my way to San Giovanni Rotondo, and found myself, early in the morning, standing in a crowd of devotees waiting for the Padre to say Mass.

I might add that when the Saint finally entered, the first thought that struck me was: "my God: he is in *samādhi*!" The Vedic term refers to a supra-conscious state transcending the confines of what we ordinarily take to be "the real world." I had witnessed *samādhi* states in India; and that is how Padre Pio appeared to me when he made his way to the altar, led by another priest.

For the next three days I hungrily seized every opportunity to experience the presence of the Saint. I realized that I was face to face with a perfect man: and that, most assuredly, is a never-to-be-forgotten experience. And childish as it may sound to many, I have not the slightest doubt that any worthy petition we make to such a Saint in our heart will receive a response. So too it is the so-called common people who seemed to understand this very well, and in fact testified to this conviction, for instance by traveling long distances to visit this "man of God."

But whereas St. Padre Pio was beloved and honored beyond measure by these "common folks," it is sad to say that such was by no means the rule among the "princes of the Church," most of whom, it seems, did not deem it worth their while to so much as set foot in San Giovanni. Some were even antagonistic towards the Saint, to the point of forbidding him to answer letters!

Getting back to Padre Pio: there is reason to believe that he ranks high among the saints of the Church. He happens in fact to be the only priest in history to have carried the stigmata: the five wounds of Christ, which came to him "out of the blue" on a Friday when he was saying Mass, and vanished again on a Friday fifty years later to the day. One might add that Padre Pio died two days after the stigmata disappeared: it had evidently been his mission thus to bear witness to Christ.

And bear witness he did! It seems that hardly a day passed during his later years without an occurrence of some kind bearing the marks of the miraculous. It is widely recognized, for example, among those who confessed to Padre Pio, that he seemed to know beforehand what each had done. For instance, one of his penitents reports that on his way to confession he inadvertently broke the mandatory fast by helping himself to some grapes: after finishing his confession, the Saint asked him: "What about those grapes?" There is abundant evidence in the archives of Padre Pio testifying to the unequivocally "miraculous" in such matters as prophecy, healing, and bilocation, to mention perhaps the most frequent categories.

The point I would make is that a saint such as Padre Pio can rightly be seen as a living exemplification of spiritual truth. Asked, for example, whether the Blessed Virgin had ever visited him in his cell: "I don't recall that she has ever left" was his reply. This is what fascinated me so greatly: where *we* read books and speculate, the saint *sees* and *knows*, because he lives *in Christ* and *Christ lives in him*: it is as simple as that. So too, we who are far from sainthood are enabled, through contact with a saint, to attain a kind of vicarious knowledge of spiritual truths, which appears to be a step above "mere theory"; and for my part, I will take an hour in the presence of St. Padre Pio over a year in the finest library.

To those, moreover, who might bemoan the fact that St. Padre Pio is no longer in the world, let me point out that they need not be sad. It happens namely that the good Padre is nearer to us at this very moment than if he were still in San Giovanni: we can in fact, at any time, commune with him, here and now, just for the asking. As in all matters Christian, however, the ineluctable requisite is *faith*.

∼

Having had quite a lot to say regarding *sādhus* of the Vedic kind, we have ended with a brief look at a Christian Saint to exhibit both the similarity as well as the profound difference between the two: for needless to say, whereas both are distinctly "supra-human" and glorious in the extreme, they are so in radically different ways. Where in the Maharshi we sense the majesty of *ātma*—the God whom "*no man has seen at any time*"—in St. Padre Pio we "see" Christ, who seems to make Himself well-nigh visible in His saints.

The question arises thus: when we look upon a consummate Christian saint, whom do we see? Is it Padre Pio, say, or is it Christ Himself? It appears to me that one can answer either way, because the Christian Eschaton—like the Vedantic—appears likewise to be, finally, a state of "nonduality," of *advaita*: only in this case that *advaita* relates, not to *ātma*, but to Christ.

Think of Sri Ramana Maharshi, and think of St. Padre Pio: where, in the Maharshi, we sense the Himalayan majesty of *ātma*—the God whom "*no man shall see and live*," corresponding in Christian terms to *God the Father*—in St. Padre Pio we catch a glimpse of *Christ* manifesting Himself in the Saint.

A GLOSSARY OF SANSKRIT TERMS

advaita — The term literally signifies "nonduality" and is used to characterize the ultimate mode of *vedānta*.

āshram — A hermitage or monastery.

ātman — The ultimate Self or Soul as well as the supreme Reality, which are declared in *advaita* Vedanta to be one and the same.

āvatāra — Often translated as "incarnation," the term is used in reference to human manifestations of God such as *Rāma* or *Krishna*.

bhakti — Love of God. The term is used in reference to the devotional modes of Vedic religion, conceived as the worship of God in human form.

brahman — The Absolute or Supreme Reality or Godhead.

cakra — A spiritual center known to yogic anatomy.

chitta — Mind.

chittavrittinirodha — Literally "the uprooting of mental modifications"; this is the classical definition of *yoga*.

darśana — One of the six classical forms of Vedic "knowing."

dharma — Religion, broadly speaking.

gerua	The orange color of the *sādhu*'s robes.
guru	The teacher or spiritual master who transmits the requisite "spark" for the practice of *yoga* to the disciple.
ishta devāta	God as conceived or worshiped in a given human form.
jiva	The individual human soul, said to be in essence identical to *ātman*.
jivanmukta	Literally one who is fully "liberated," the term refers to a *yogin* whose body has survived the attainment of supreme Enlightenment.
karma	Action in general, or its effects.
māyā	A state of ignorance affecting post-Edenic mankind, which can only be removed by way of the *chittavrittinirodha*.
moksha	Supreme enlightenment, tantamount to the destruction of *māyā*.
neti, neti	Literally "*not so, not so*," a double negation used frequently in Vedic literature to remind us of our subjection to *māyā*.
nirodha	Literally "uprooting," the Sanskrit *rodha* being cognate to our noun "root."
nirvāna	Literally the word means, more or less, "blowing out," and refers in particular to the *yogic* extinction of the *māyā*-bound human subject.
purusha	In its Vedantic connotation the term refers to *ātman*, the supreme Self.

rishi	The term refers to an accomplished master, especially to those mentioned in the Vedic texts.
sādhu	A monastic who has dedicated his life to the quest of God.
samādhi	A superconscious state attainable through *yoga*, especially the supreme state resulting from *chittavrittinirodha*.
sanātana dharma	Literally "the eternal religion," a Hindu term referring to the Vedic religion.
sannyāsi	A monk dedicated to the practice of *yoga*.
vedānta	The highest of the six *darśanas*.
vritti	A term used to refer to the modifications of the mind.
yoga	The traditional means of spiritual ascent indigenous to the Vedic tradition.
yogi	A practitioner of *yoga*.

INDEX OF NAMES

Abhishiktananda, Swami 41-59, 71
Adam 62, 70, 82-3, 85
Anandamayi Ma, Sri 3 fn.
Aquinas, St. Thomas 31, 65-6, 87, 91, 98
Arjuna 13, 24
Arnold, Edwin 19 fn., 59
Augustine, St. 3, 26 fn., 28-9, 35, 39, 89, 91, 97

Balthasar, Hans Urs von 7, 17, 21, 29, 58, 86, 87
Black, Max 2
Borella, Jean 29, 93-9
Buddha, Gautama 12, 19 fn., 55, 57
Bultmann, Rudolf 95

Catherine of Siena, St. 3, 20, 88
Clement of Alexandria 9
Coomaraswamy, Ananda 81, 83

Descartes, René 93
du Boulay, Shirley 41 fn., 42, 44, 46

Einstein, Albert 92

Gregory of Nyssa, St. 28-9, 34
Guénon, René 73, 93, 94

Hugh of St. Victor 91, 97

John, St. 3, 40, 61, 86, 89

Krishna, Sri 13, 22 fn., 24, 62

Le Saux, Henri *See* Abhishiktananda.

Meister Eckhart 5, 6, 8, 30-9, 78-9, 87, 90
Monchanin, Jules 44, 48, 49
Müller, Max 54

Oldmeadow, Harry 55, 56, 58 fn.
Osborne, Arthur 44

Padre Pio, St. 101-4
Paine, Scott Randall 7
Pantaenus 9 fn.
Patanjali 9
Parmenides 10, 11 fn.
Paul, St. 4, 9 fn., 21, 27, 53, 68
Peter, St. 86
Pius XII, Pope 95
Plato 28 fn., 93, 94, 100

Ramakrishna, Sri 1, 2
Ramana Maharshi, Sri 12, 23, 44-5, 46, 49, 50, 57, 64
Reginald of Piperno 31, 87

Schuon, Frithjof 21, 73-5, 76-8, 79, 80, 86

Shankaracharya 20, 48
Socrates 11

Tagore, Rabindranath 1

Vivekananda, Swami 2

ABOUT THE AUTHOR

WOLFGANG SMITH was born in Vienna in 1930. At age eighteen he graduated from Cornell University with majors in physics, mathematics, and philosophy. At age twenty he took his master's degree in physics at Purdue University, subsequently contributing a theoretical solution to the re-entry problem for space flight while working as an aerodynamicist at Bell Aircraft Corporation. After taking his doctorate in mathematics at Columbia University he pursued a career as professor of mathematics at M.I.T., U.C.L.A., and Oregon State University until his retirement in 1992.

Notwithstanding his professional engagement with physics and mathematics, Wolfgang Smith is at heart a philosopher in the traditional sense. Early in life he became deeply attracted to the Platonist and Neoplatonist schools, and ultimately undertook extensive sojourns in India and the Himalayan regions to contact such vestiges of ancient tradition as could still be found. One of the basic lessons he learned by way of these encounters is that there actually exist higher sciences in which man himself plays the part not merely of the observer, but of the "scientific instrument": i.e., becomes himself, as it were, the "microscope" or "telescope" by which he is enabled to access normally invisible reaches of the integral cosmos. By the same token, Smith came to recognize the stringent limitations to which our contemporary sciences are subject by virtue of their "extrinsic" *modus operandi*: the folly of presuming to fathom the depths of the universe, having barely scratched the surface in the discovery of man himself.

Following his retirement from academic life, Smith devoted himself to the publication of books missioned to correct the fallacies of contemporary scientistic belief by way of insights derived from the perennial wisdom of mankind. These works focus primarily on foundational problems in quantum theory and the no less challenging quandaries related to the problem of visual perception. The key to the overall puzzle, according to Smith, is to be found in the long lost cosmology of antiquity, which conceives of the integral cosmos as tripartite—even as man himself is traditionally viewed as a composite of *corpus*, *anima*, and *spiritus*.

The Philos-Sophia Initiative Foundation has produced a feature documentary on the life and work of Dr. Smith, *The End of Quantum Reality*, which is available on disc and digital platforms worldwide. Visit theendofquantumreality.com for more information.

www.ingramcontent.com/pod-product-compliance
Lightning Source LLC
Chambersburg PA
CBHW020655060526
44119CB00089B/387/J